FAMILY VIOLENCE

FAMILY VIOLENCE

The Compassionate Church Responds

Melissa A. Miller
Foreword by Carolyn Holderread Heggen

HERALD PRESS
Waterloo, Ontario
Scottdale, Pennsylvania

Canadian Cataloging-in-Publication Data
Miller, Melissa, 1954-
    Family violence : the compassionate church responds

Includes bibliographical references.
ISBN 0-8361-3654-3

1. Church work with problem families. 2. Family violence—Religious
aspects—Christianity. 3. Pastoral counseling. 4. Problem families—
Counseling of. I. Title.

BV4438.5.M55 1994 261.8'3587   C93-095464-5

The paper used in this publication is recycled and meets the minimum
requirements of American National Standard for Information
Sciences—Permanence of Paper for Printed Library Materials, ANSI
Z39.48-1984.

FAMILY VIOLENCE
Copyright © 1994 by Herald Press, Waterloo, Ont. N2L 6H7
    Published simultaneously in the United States by Herald Press,
    Scottdale, Pa. 15683. All rights reserved
Library of Congress Catalog Number: 93-80269
International Standard Book Number: 0-8361-3654-3
Printed in the United States of America
Book design by Gwen M. Stamm
Cover design by Ingrid Hess

3 4 5 6 7 8 9 10 02 01 00 99 98 97

To all the saints, young and old,
female and male, of Mannheim Mennonite Church:

Among you I find
acceptance
laughter and play
commitment to justice-making
compassion
and keen desire to follow God's call.

Contents

Foreword

IN RECENT YEARS we have been forced to admit publicly what many have privately known since childhood—Christian homes are not immune to violence and abuse. Even denominations that have highlighted the nonviolent teachings of Jesus have had to acknowledge domestic violence and abuse among their own members.

Some of us working in the field of family violence have observed that Christian theology and certain biblical teachings include the belief that God intends men to dominate and women and children to submit, that children are inherently evil and must have their wills broken, that marriages be preserved at all costs, that suffering is a Christian virtue, and that Christians must quickly forgive those who sin against them.

It is unsettling to acknowledge that children growing up in Christian homes are no safer from violence and abuse than children in non-Christian homes. It is disturbing to know that distortions of some Christian teachings may actually put women at risk of being battered by their husbands.

Looking at this issue is difficult for all of us. For some, it evokes disturbing memories of having watched helplessly as a child while a parent or sibling was humiliated, shamed, or beaten. For others, haunting memories of their own childhood violation surface when the issue is discussed. Rather than malign their parents or face their own inner pain, some adult survivors minimize and discredit the violence committed against them. They may insist, "It can't be that bad; I was whipped and put down as a kid, but I turned out fine."

Some persons repress and forget many of the cruel and humiliating things done to them as children. As Alice Miller has helped us understand, when we are abused as children and not allowed to grieve over the violence committed against us, we numb our hearts to survive. Many of us are now sensitive to the problem of family violence. Some know their own potential for violence against those they love. They want to learn new, life-enhancing ways of relating. But while feeling uncomfortable with their harsh methods of parenting, many don't know any other ways of relating to children. Others have heard the painful stories of friends within the congregation who have been affected by abuse and want to walk compassionately and redemptively with them. Many individuals and congregations are asking for guidance and resources as they together face this critical congregational matter.

In *Family Violence*, Melissa Miller has given us an important tool for understanding and confronting this urgent issue. As a family therapist, with broad professional training and experience, she speaks with authority and insight. As a spiritual person, she envisions the congregation as the healing body of Christ for both survivors and offenders. She calls forth the best in local congregations while giving Christians practical guidelines for holding each other accountable and becoming channels of grace for one another. Using Scripture to highlight issues related to family violence, Miller helps us make the biblical stories our own by her insightful reflections and questions for discussion.

Individuals and groups will find in *Family Violence* a sensitive, practical resource. The book will be useful for understanding the complex notion of interpersonal power and ways such power can be so easily and destructively misused within families.

I pray that Miller's book will help many among us identify and acknowledge the shame and suffering we experienced as children so we may grieve for our own pain and not pass it on to our children.

As Miller helps us understand, we must stop seeing violence as a normal, acceptable part of life. The well-being of our children, our communities, and our very planet depends on learning gentler ways of living together. Global peace may seem elusive, but let us begin with loving, nonviolent responses to our children and spouses in our individual homes and personal relationships.

   —*Carolyn Holderread Heggen,*
    Albuquerque, New Mexico, author of
    Sexual Abuse in Christian Homes and Churches

Acknowledgments

A<small>S I WROTE</small> this book, I was surrounded by a tremendous "cloud of witnesses." The support of my community made the arduous task of writing about this painful subject much more manageable.

Mennonite Central Committee (MCC) provided a grant which made this project possible. Dave Worth (MCC Ontario), Esther Epp-Tiessen (MCC Canada), and Tina Mast Burnett (MCC U.S.), in addition to contributing to this book, continue to provide perceptive leadership as churches respond to domestic violence and sexual abuse. Financial support for this project was provided by the Hallman family: Peter, Susan, Jim, and Tom.

Glenn Brubacher (executive director of Shalom Counselling Services) offered administrative support that was both encouraging and empowering.

Many of the counselors from Shalom joined with a number of others to form a reader's group. These people were invited to critique the text because of their perspectives as pastor, survivor, Christian educator, offender, theologian, justice-maker, and writer. Their feedback on the first draft immeasurably improved the final copy. The reader's group included Bruce Brillinger, Glenn Brubacher, Tina Mast Burnett, Jurgen Czechowsky, Helen Epp, Esther Epp-Tiessen, Marie Marshall Fortune, Lydia Harder, Carolyn Holderread Heggen, Marcia Metzler Holsopple, Johanna Jamnik, Jeanne Kelly, Ruth Anne Laverty, Delphine Martin, Alan Miller, Dean Peachey, Ron Rempel, Janine Schultz, Eleanor Snyder, and Dave Worth.

Carol Lichti was unfailingly pleasant and competent as she swiftly transformed the manuscript from my (sometimes illegible) handwriting to typed copy. Herald Press, represented by editor Michael King, was prompt to publish the book, demonstrating commitment to provide resources to deal with family abuse.

I am indebted to three courageous women, who lead all of us in responding to the tragedies of sexual abuse and violence within families: Marie Marshall Fortune, Carolyn Holderread Heggen, and Ruth Krall.

The Women's Group, in the persons of Esther Epp-Tiessen, Anna Hemmendinger, and Ann Weber Becker, was an ongoing source of companionship, humor, and restoration.

Julie Weber caught most of my moments of teary insecurity, listened sensitively, and by doing so, enabled me to move from despair to serenity. Doris Gascho continues to affirm and instruct, gently and quietly, guiding me towards God's inner call.

Chris Derstine, Phil Martin, and their children, Suzanne and Simon, are cherished friends and supporters. Together they create a family which models mutually empowering love.

My biological family (centered in my parents, Eugene and Sara Miller) and my acquired family (centered in my parents-in-law, LeRoy and Lois Peachey) are important sources of learning and love.

Finally, my husband, Dean Peachey, and my son, Daniel, form the day-to-day context in which I experience family. They know me and my uses of power intimately. Still they offer me steadfast love, a challenge to be faithful, and a secure home.

With a full heart, I thank you all.

Author's Preface

THIS BOOK CAME about because of two men who, from their positions of power, nudged me toward the task. Dave Worth, director of Mennonite Central Committee Ontario, and Glenn Brubacher, executive director of Shalom Counselling, prodded and pushed and encouraged until I submitted a proposal that they gladly supported.

I hesitated partly because the work of counseling survivors and offenders of family violence had taken a toll, and I was weary in spirit. In retrospect, writing the book was good medicine, for I was given the opportunity to put words to my inner journey, and experience healing.

As the waves of revelations and open discussion of family violence roll over the churches, it seems vital to offer a tool to aid congregations in responding. Terms like *power, abuse,* and *violence* are not normally included when we consider the Christian family. However, for too long too many hurting persons have had to struggle alone. It is hoped that this book will enable congregations to learn about and respond sensitively to the many individuals who suffer because of the abuse of power within families.

I am deeply indebted to the individuals who shared their stories with me and gave me permission to share them with you. Where requested, names were changed to preserve anonymity.

Throughout the book, I refer to *victim/survivors*, *offenders*, and *witnesses*. A victim is an individual who has suffered from abuse; a survivor is an individual who recognizes the victimization and is on the healing path. An offender is an individual who used power in harmful, abusive ways and in doing so damaged a family member. A witness is someone who does not have direct experience with family violence, yet is called to witness it and who may respond by "bearing witness."

I recognize that an exploration of family violence will cause readers to examine their own family relationships, past and present. I do not expect all individuals to label themselves as survivors or offenders or both. However, given the history of power abuses common in our churches, society, and families, I expect many readers will encounter unresolved hurts of varying intensity. I hope this book may encourage you to seek resolution of those pains, and that you will find support to do so in your church community or, when appropriate, with a therapist.

Some readers may feel disturbed when pondering past uses of power and wonder if others perceived them as abusive. May you also find in your church community a supportive place to resolve your past.

May our gracious God direct each individual struggling with the abuse of power toward healing.

—*Melissa A. Miller*
Kitchener, Ontario

1

Setting the Stage: Understanding Power in the Family

"CAN I HELP?" my son inquired.

I hesitatingly replied, "Okay." I had just begun to rearrange the photos of family and friends that decorated the kitchen bulletin board. I had a plan and was not truly open to altering it.

As expected, Daniel's ideas were different from mine. Tension built as I overrode his suggestions and placed the pictures according to my scheme.

Finally he exploded, "You think you're the government or something. You're always telling people what to do."

Surprised by his sharp insight, I laughed. The tension broke and we resumed our work, with "the government" being more accommodating.

Introduction

We begin our study of family violence with a consideration of family health. What is the family intended to do and be? What is God's design for families? How can the Scriptures guide us in family relationships? What can we learn from the social sciences? By addressing the appropriate use of power in this chapter, we set the context for our discussion in subsequent chapters of the abuse of power.

I believe God does not intend power abuses to be a normal part of family relationships. While conflict, misunderstandings, arguments, and anger are all appropriate and normal parts of family life, violence is not. Violence is sin.

Imagine a Family

Family. Reflect for a moment on the word. What images develop in your mind as you think about families?

Does the nuclear family come to mind? Two parents and one to three kids? All walking into church neatly dressed, looking happy and confident?

Or do you think of an extended family, dozens of people, different ages, all descended from one set of ancestors, gathered to celebrate a family event such as a wedding—with shared history, laughter, bonds, simmering tensions that may or may not boil openly?

Perhaps you consider a fractured family. A strained or severed family relationship.

Or you might imagine an individual without family ties, feeling lonely and unanchored.

Maybe your thoughts go to a church family. A gathering of individuals with a common belief system, common commitments, common rituals.

Our response to the word *family* is shaped by our experiences with families—our first families, the families we create as adults, our friends' families, our church families. Our awareness of power uses and abuses is also rooted in those same experiences.

What Is a Family?

There are many varieties of families. Each person enters the world in the same way, through the uniting of one male and one female. Subsequent family experiences, even within North America, vary considerably.

Some children grow up living with those same two parents. Some parents do not marry, and may or may not nurture the child they have created. Adopted children are nurtured by adults other than their biological parents. Death or divorce alters the constellation; some parents are singly raising their children. Remarriage creates another kind of family—if children are involved, it is sometimes called a blended family. Then there are families with more than two significant adults—perhaps including grandparents, other extended family members, or close friends—rearing the children.

Webster's dictionary defines *family,* as among other things, "the basic unit in society having at its nucleus two or more adults living together and cooperating in the care and rearing of their own or adopted children." This definition fails to recognize the many one-parent families who have existed throughout history. However, it does focus on the family's key function of caring for the young. Yet what about couples who do not have children? Adult couples who cohabit are family to each other.

It does appear that at least two people are required to make a family. And abuse occurs when at least two people are present— a perpetrator and a victim.

This is not intended to devalue the worth of individuals or people who live singly. In fact, one mission of the church is to look beyond biological connections. Recall the way Jesus redefined family. While he was speaking to a large crowd one day, he was told that his mother and brothers were waiting outside to speak to him. Gesturing to his disciples, Jesus proclaimed, "Here are my mother and my brothers! For whoever does the will of my Father in heaven is my brother and sister and mother." (Matt. 12:46-50)

In the same manner, we name other Christians as sister and brother, affirming the new family that God creates. It is a task of the church to value each person as an equally worthy daughter or son of God.

Power in the Family

It is essential that we identify sources of power within the family. We can only understand how power is abused and work toward its correct use if we acknowledge and identify power in the family.

Many of us are uncomfortable with such a discussion. We think of power in negative ways. We link power with domination and manipulation; we do not want to describe ourselves in such a way. We must rethink our understanding of power.

In understanding personal power, it is useful to apply the following assumptions.

1. Power can also be thought of as resources or privilege.

2. Power can be considered opposite to vulnerability.

3. Power itself is not good or bad. Good and bad relate to the way in which power is used.

4. An individual's power or vulnerability is always in relationship to the power or vulnerability of others.

(The above assumptions are based on material from *Clergy Sexual Misconduct Workshop Manual*, p. 38.)

Using these assumptions, let us consider an example. In the story which opens this chapter, my son correctly identified the power dynamic between us. To return to the assumptions—

1. I was exercising my power (or privilege) by insisting he place the pictures according to my plan.

2. He was vulnerable to my directives because I possessed greater physical strength, and I was controlling where he could or could not place the photos.

3. He protested my use of power. He wanted to use his own power to place pictures. I misused my parental power by denying him the opportunity to share in the task.

4. As stated previously, Daniel had less power. He used his voice (one form of personal power) to seek a change in the way I was using power. By doing so, he gained more power. I responded by accommodating his ideas about picture placement, so that the experience became more empowering for Daniel.

We will continue to reflect on power and its correct uses and sinful abuses throughout this study. We will apply biblical stories and other references to better develop an understanding of the healthy use of power. God calls us to use our power and resources in ways that empower and nurture those around us.

Healthy Families Nurture

Nurture is present in healthy families, whether they be church families, families with children, extended families, or child-free families. Each person in the family experiences nurture, affectionate care, and attention. Nurturance is also growth-oriented—the individuals are being nurtured to grow.

Such growth is perhaps easiest to observe with children. When provided with shelter and clothing, food and tender care, children grow physically, emotionally, and spiritually. It is the parents who set the tone for the family, and on them rests the responsibility for the nurture and training of the children.

Growth does not end at age eighteen or when children leave home, however. Our family, friend, and church relationships continue to nurture us as we age. We cease to grow physically, but we grow in our emotional and spiritual abilities. Healthy families nurture.

The Bible and Nurturance

How does the Bible guide us in nurturing family relationships? What instructions do we find in the Bible to shape family relations based on nurture, affectionate care, and attention?

In some ways the Bible offers limited instructions on nurturance. When we look at families in the Bible, we are given little information about how the children were raised, or about relationships between spouses. This is a reminder of how the biblical writings were shaped by the particular societies in which they occurred.

We must recognize those cultural differences as we reflect on biblical messages regarding family relationships. Each culture has its expectations of correct family relationships and its understanding of the value of human life.

These cultural differences emerge even within a few generations living in the same country. I recall visiting with my grandfather one day. He asked about my work. I told him I was leading a discussion on self-esteem later that day.

"You probably didn't think too much about self-esteem in your earlier years, did you?" I wondered aloud.

"No," he replied. "We were too busy keeping the wolves away from the door."

I was struck by the differences between three generations. I have never known poverty so stark as to make me use the metaphor my grandfather used. Nor have my parents. The haunting phrase reminds me of the families who have little energy beyond that used in the struggle for daily bread.

Much of the Bible was probably written in a similar setting of struggle for daily bread. The lack of helpful family life instructions must be understood in this context.

Despite cultural differences, we still find biblical themes that can be expanded and linked with current social science information to offer us healthy, Christian guidelines for family relationships.

A Bible Story—God's Response to Human Loneliness

Consider the lovely poetry that surrounds the creation of the first family.

> But for the man, there was not found a helper as his partner.
> So the Lord God caused a deep sleep to fall upon the man, and he slept; then he took one of his ribs and closed up its place with flesh. And the rib that the Lord God had taken from the man he made into a woman and brought her to the man.
> Then the man said,
> "This at last is bone of my bones
> and flesh of my flesh;
> this one shall be called Woman
> for out of Man this one was taken."
> Therefore a man leaves his father and his mother and clings to his wife, and they become one flesh. And the man and his wife were both naked, and were not ashamed. (Gen. 2:20b-25)

Reflections on the Bible Story

1. The man in the story was lonely. Even though he had God and later a garden full of animals, his loneliness persisted. God responded by creating another human being for companionship. Only then was the man's loneliness remedied.

2. God models nurturance by sensing Adam's loneliness and responding to his needs for human companionship.

3. Deep, binding intimacy was created between humans. The

rich imagery of "bone of my bones," "one flesh" and "naked . . . and not ashamed" expresses a life-sustaining connection.

4. Mutuality, equality, and respect underpinned the relationships, particularly when set alongside of the Genesis 1 account of creation. Eve is Adam's helper—not a subordinate but a strong companion, even a redeemer or savior. (The same Hebrew word is used to describe God in Psalms 121:1-2, which affirms that "my help comes from the Lord." The word translated "help" is never used to suggest subordinate or inferior.)

5. In that context of mutual respect and equality, the humans could be naked and unashamed. That is, they could be completely vulnerable, trusting, and peaceful with each other.

Making the Bible Story Our Story

1. We need intimate connections with other people. We do not require a spouse, but we must have companions whose presence speaks to the yearnings known to Adam as loneliness.

2. This scene from the garden points us to God's intentions for family relationships. Spouses are to respond to each other with equality, respect and joy.

3. Parents respond to children's needs as God did to Adam's, with sensitivity and nurturance.

Jesus and Nurture

A similar nurturance can be found in Jesus' remarks about children.

> Truly I tell you, unless you change and become like children, you will never enter the kingdom of heaven. Whoever becomes humble like this child is the greatest in the kingdom of heaven. Whoever welcomes one such child in my name welcomes me (Matt. 18:3-5).

We can almost see a young child basking in the glow of Jesus' affection. Jesus' famous golden rule can also be applied to families. "Do to others as you would have them do to you" (Matt. 7:12).

Nurture and Self-Esteem

Let us return to the concept of nurture. A child who is nurtured will develop healthy self-esteem. Self-esteem means the ability to value oneself.

Self-esteem affects all of our actions and relationships. People with high self-esteem can voice their wants and needs clearly, and respond to others from a position of strength.

A woman who likes herself can move confidently in the world, unhampered by overblown concerns about what others think. A man who likes himself will be able to listen patiently and respectfully to another's point of view, not fearful that his opinion must be defended with his whole self. A child who sees herself as a treasure will be able to take manageable risks, learning from successes as well as failures without being crushed.

Building Self-Esteem

How is self-esteem built? Linda Tschirhart Sanford and Mary Ellen Donovan (writing in *Women and Self-Esteem,* pp. 38-54) develop a useful understanding of the necessary requirements for building self-esteem in children. They list five things—significance, competence, connectedness balanced by separateness, a realistic view of oneself and the world, and ethics and values.

Using their model, let us consider the categories in more detail. I offer two examples in each category, one from my experience as a child and one from my current family.

1. *Significance.* People need to know that they are valued and important. Parents convey this to children by verbal and nonverbal messages. An infant who receives food, comfort, and dry clothes promptly will gain a secure sense of his significance. A woman who is listened to, respected, and affirmed by family members will feel significant.

Examples

• One of my favorite memories is the care with which my mother helped us celebrate birthdays. We were invited to choose the menu for our birthday dinner and to place an order for the flavor and decorations of the cake. We were relieved of daily chores. This gave the message that I was valued and my birthday was a special time for recalling that value.

• One evening I wearily put my three-year-old to bed. I

rushed him through his bedtime routine and left abruptly. I was displeased (but not surprised) to hear his protests. I tried to ignore them, but his sad cries broke through my resistance. Frustrated with the constant tasks of parenting, I retraced my steps, opened the door, crossed the room, and stretched out on the bed beside him. Joy replaced his sorrow. He curved his arms around my neck and exclaimed, "Oh, Mama, you're my best friend ever." My irritation melted in the warmth of his love.

He clearly signaled my significance in his life.

2. *Competence.* Self-esteem grows when an individual knows his gifts and can confidently use them. Parents who encourage children to experiment with opportunities and who support them as they develop their skills set the stage for confident children. Spouses can affirm and support each other's talents.

Examples

• Growing up in the country in the middle of a large family, I felt incompetent when it came to butchering chickens and sewing clothes. I developed and was appreciated for my ability to put the baby to sleep and to run the loads of laundry through the wringer washer.

• Like music to my ears are my husband's affirmations.

"This is tasty bread you made."

"You did a really good job of leading the congregation in worship today."

"You are so patient in your explanations to Daniel."

3. *Connectedness balanced by separation.* Children need to have a sense of belonging to a particular family. They also need freedom to move from that unit. It has been well expressed in the popular quote, "There are two things we can give our children. One is roots, the other wings." Adults also benefit from being connected to, and separated from, a particular family.

Examples

• My parents encouraged connectedness by family fun times, like Sunday afternoon baseball games, mountain hikes, and Easter baskets filled with sweet treats. The more mundane activities of eating dinner and planting the garden together were also important.

A message my parents sent regarding separateness related to our beds. They made sure each child had his or her own bed. Even though we shared the public space during the day, we had private space at night.

• I value the opportunity to be separate from my family responsibilities as I respond to stimulating experiences outside the home. At the same time, it is important for me to maintain the connection with my loved ones. I do this by regularly phoning home to hear what is happening in the lives of those at home and to tell what I am experiencing while I am away.

4. *Realism*. Children need to develop an accurate view of themselves. Parents can err on either of two extremes here. They may give the child the message that she is a perfect princess without fault or flaw. Or they may not adequately affirm the child's strengths, focusing only on his weaknesses. Children need to know that they are human, not perfect; they require guidance to help them deal with their flaws. Adults, too, benefit from honest feedback; it enables them to keep a realistic view of themselves.

In addition to gaining a realistic view of himself, a child needs to develop a realistic sense of the world. What are genuine dangers, and where is it safe to take risks?

Children develop their view of the world in part by the limits their parents set. As parents guide their children, they teach about consequences. The child learns about how the world responds to certain actions. The parents are teachers as they expose these connections to their children.

Examples

• My mother insisted we could not own or ride bicycles on the narrow twisting road where we lived. She likely had a realistic view of how dangerous that would be.

As we each became old enough to drive, my dad patiently went through the learning steps with us. He taught us to drive first on the automatic and then the standard transmission, coached us through our driving tests, paid the insurance and repair bills. In short, he helped us develop a realistic sense of the dangers and opportunities available to us as car drivers.

• I regularly ask my spouse to edit my writing. Because of his feedback, I am better able to see the flaws and strengths of the writing.

5. *Ethics and values.* Children need a value base from which to make ethical decisions. Parents will be a child's first teachers of what is right and wrong. A child's first moral code is based on the model she observes in her parents. Adults use their ethics and values as the foundation of their lifestyle. A person with such a value base experiences self-esteem as he makes decisions consistent with his moral code.

Examples

• My parents taught by word and example a number of ethic values I follow today—Christian faith, the value of service to others, respect for all people.

• I recently talked with my husband about a number of financial decisions. We share an understanding that we are managers of the resources (financial and otherwise) that God has entrusted to us. This Christian value guides us in the management of our finances.

Conclusions

In summary then, we can establish a number of principles regarding healthy families.

1. Nurture is a key function of families. Physical, emotional, and spiritual care should be provided for individuals' needs.

2. Families are base camps for the development and maintenance of self-esteem. Positive self-esteem enables one to live life to the fullest. When self-esteem is high, we are best able to be the person God created us to be.

3. Healthy family relationships acknowledge that each person is an equally blessed child of God. Mutual respect is woven through all interactions.

Prayer

Dear God,

We thank you for lovingly inviting us into your family. We bring our family experiences, past and present, into our walk with you. We bring our hurts and joys. Guide us into healthy family relationships today. Amen.

Discussion Questions

1. Consider the discussion of the five necessary requirements for building self-esteem in children—significance, competence, connectedness balanced by separateness, a realistic view of oneself and the world, and ethics and values.

Give examples of where these factors were present or absent during your growing-up years.

How do these factors operate in your current family?

2. Consider the discussion of power and vulnerability. Take some time to identify your personal power and vulnerability. Where do you experience yourself as more powerful than others? Where do you experience yourself as being more vulnerable than others? In your group, note any differences in the responses by men and women.

3. Consider the discussion of the Bible story. At what points do you agree or disagree with the author's interpretation of how this Bible story applies to family relationships?

4. How does or can the church community encourage us to nurture each other?

Resources

Faber, Adele and Elaine Mazlish, *How to Talk So Kids Will Listen and Listen So Kids Will Talk.*

Fortune, Marie M., "Power and Vulnerability," *Clergy Misconduct: Sexual Abuse in the Ministerial Relationship.*

Poling, James Newton, *The Abuse of Power: A Theological Problem.*

Sanford, Linda Tschirhart and Mary Ellen Donovan, *Women and Self-Esteem.*

(Note: See Bibliography for more complete bibliographic data.)

2

The Abuse of Physical Power

JANIE RAN from her father's blows. She knew from past experience that he could hurt her badly. She ran, vainly trying to ward off further assault. He followed her down the lane and into the small forest. When he caught her, he struck her over and over. The belt stung her flesh until she was numb.

Janie fled toward the house. He caught her before she reached the steps and beat her again. She fell to the ground, unable to walk because of the pain. He continued to whip her. She writhed up the steps while his blows stormed over her.

Her mother screamed, "Stop it!"

Eventually he did. Janie dragged herself into her room and locked the door.

* * * * * * * * * *

Introduction

The abuse of physical power in family relationships is discouragingly prevalent. Christian families do not have reason to be proud of their record in this regard. In fact, in too many Christian families, physical punishment is linked to God's directives. Then the survivor has to recover both from the physical blows delivered by a loved one and the mistaken belief that God willed such abuse.

Physical violence occurs in a variety of family relationships. Husbands assault wives. Though it occurs less frequently, a wife may assault her husband. Children are beaten by their parents. Elderly parents are abused by their adult children and other caregivers. We will focus primarily on the abuse of children and women in this chapter, with a brief discussion of the abuse of husbands and the elderly.

This is not intended to minimize the abuse of the elderly or the abuse of husbands. The abuse of physical power is wrong whatever the circumstances. Offenders need to be held accountable for their transgressions.

In our society, wife and child abuse occurs most frequently. Literature and research is readily available on the subject of wife and child abuse; it is more difficult to find studies on other physical abuse. We hope that the dynamics we consider as we explore wife and child abuse will instruct us as we consider other kinds of physically abusive family relationships.

Definition

Physical abuse includes hitting, burning, slapping, pinching, whipping, biting, or otherwise physically injuring another person, whether or not bruises, broken bones, or internal injuries result (*Allies in Healing*, p. 232, by Laura Davis). The destruction of property or pets is another form of abuse.

A Bible Story—Jephthah's Sacrifice of His Daughter

Let us turn to a Bible story to set the context for our discussion. In Judges 11 we read the account of Jephthah's sacrifice of his daughter. The story occurs during the period of time when the Israelites were fighting to maintain their territory in the Promised Land, from 1200-1050 B.C. The book of Judges is filled with stories of brutal battles, heroes and heroines, cruel deaths, and unthinkable tragedies.

Jephthah was a warrior, a commander of the Israelites as they fought the Ammonites. One day, as Jephthah was about to begin a battle, the Spirit of the Lord came upon him and Jephthah vowed

> "[Lord], if you will give the Ammonites into my hand, then whoever comes out of the doors of my house to meet me, when I return victorious from the Ammonites, shall be the Lord's, to be offered up by me as a burnt offering."
>
> The Lord gave [the Ammonites] into [Jephthah's] hand. . . . Jephthah came to his home at Mispah; and there was his daughter, coming out to meet him with timbrels and with dancing. [Jephthah] tore his clothes and said, "Alas, my daughter! You have brought me very low; you have become the cause of great trouble to me. For I have opened the mouth to the Lord, and I cannot take back my vow" (vv. 31-35).

The daughter submitted to her fate, and requested two months to roam the hills and weep with her friends, mourning that she would never marry. Jephthah consented. The daughter grieved with her friends, then returned home where her father sacrificed her.

Reflections on the Bible Story

This horrible story occurred in a particular cultural context which included child sacrifice as normal. Children were regularly killed to appease Molech, the god of the Ammonites. Israel was in touch with these other groups, through proximity of lands, commerce, intermarriage, and political unions. Israelites were susceptible to the belief that their God, Yahweh, desired human sacrifice.

Various Old Testament references testify to Yahweh's distaste for such sacrifice. Leviticus 18:21 and 20:2-5 prohibit the practice. The second passage warns that any parents who sacrifice their child must be stoned to death themselves. Furthermore, God declares, "If the people of the land should ever close their eyes to them, when they give of their offspring . . . and do not put them to death, I myself will set my face against them . . . and will cut them off from among their people . . . all who follow them."

Yet the temptation remained. Solomon built a high place for Molech "the abomination of the Ammonites" (1 Kings 11:7). Later Josiah desecrated a pagan god's temple so that "no one would make a son or a daughter pass through fire as an offering to Molech" (2 Kings 23:10).

The prophet Jeremiah offered a stern reproach from God, "They build the high places . . . to offer up their sons and daughters to Molech, though I did not command them, nor did it enter my mind that they should do this abomination" (Jer. 32:35).

Somehow Jephthah understood Yahweh to want such a sacrifice. Having made the vow, he felt he had no choice but to fulfill it. Still it is chilling to read the passage with no mention of God condemning the loss of this child's life.

Even taking into account the cultural acceptance of child sacrifice, we must ponder why Jephthah would make such a risky vow. After all, it was the custom for the women to come dancing to meet the triumphant warriors and welcome them home.

Then there is the account of Abraham's near sacrifice of Isaac. The angel of the Lord intervened at the last moment, commanding Abraham, "Do not lay your hand on the boy." Abraham then discovered a ram stuck in a nearby thicket, and sacrificed the animal "instead of his son" (Gen. 22:1-14). Isaac's life was preserved, but one wonders how this event affected Isaac, his relationship with his father, and his understanding of God.

Making the Bible Story Our Story

Let us consider elements of the sacrifice of Jephthah's daughter relevant for our discussion of physical violence within families.

1. The offender typically has a great deal of power, perhaps even the appearance of unlimited power over the victim. Husbands who abuse their wives physically generally control their behavior in other areas, including finances and social life. Children abused by their parents are quite controlled.

2. Jephthah linked his sacrifice of his daughter to his commitment to Yahweh. Many Christian parents believe they must strike their children because it is God's will.

3. The victim is blamed. Jephthah immediately scolds his

daughter and reproaches her for making him "very low" and causing him "great trouble." His misery seems more significant than her loss of life. She is also blamed for normal behavior that in other circumstances would have been welcomed.

4. Our culture may shape us to harm our family members. The effects of our culture may override our religious values.

5. The victims lose. It may be the ultimate loss, that of one's life. There is certainly loss of freedom, dignity, security, and wholeness. The offenders also lose, even if they never recognize their loss. Jephthah lost his only child. Abusive husbands may lose their wives and families. Abusive parents lose their children's love and trust.

Husbands Abusing Wives

The above points drawn from the biblical story apply to today's tragedy of wife abuse. Issues of power and control, blaming the victim, and misinterpretation of religious values all relate to wife abuse in Christian homes.

The Church's Shame

A pastor asked me how to counsel a couple from his church; he suspected the wife was being abused.

I called the local women's shelter to supplement my information to pass on to the pastor for his rural congregation. Midway through the conversation, I was stopped cold when the counselor said, "If she's Mennonite, she is in danger."

I was silenced and deeply troubled by her view of my church. I wanted to protest, "We're not all like that." I yearned for the opportunity to inform her of our denunciation of violence and the tangible specific supports we provide to abused wives.

But I knew I had little to offer. My denomination has responded to domestic violence through the efforts of task forces and publication of widely distributed materials. But the brave women and men actively working against domestic violence have had to struggle against the tide. I swallowed my hollow defense and pondered my shame privately. My denomination, though known around the world for its commitment to peacemaking has, like other denominations, been woefully slow to address domestic violence.

Yet this massive evil is now finally beginning to be recognized. Since the mid-1970s, women's shelters have opened in thousands of communities across North America. Generally they operate on struggling budgets, with great demands on their resources, and little or no support from local churches.

It is estimated that between one-third to two-thirds of all wives know violence at the hands of their husbands (*Battered into Submission*, pp. 28-29). We have no reason to believe that these statistics do not apply to Christian marriages.

Generally sexual and emotional abuse accompany physical abuse. In some instances there is little actual physical violence. But the husband has used violence at points in the relationship, and the wife knows he can be violent again. So even though the violence may be infrequent, she lives constantly with the threat of violence and her behavior is thereby controlled.

Abusers

Why do men abuse their wives? How can a man promise to love and care for a woman, then humiliate and mar her with physical violations?

We are looking at a complex series of factors. The simplest factor, though, is that an abuser chooses to treat his spouse violently because he has learned this abuse of power and believes he can get away with it. Husbands who choose physically to abuse their wives have been taught by family and society that this is normal behavior. Until recently, offenders did not have to experience the consequences of their abuse. Cultural acceptance of wife abuse is centuries old. The phrase "rule of thumb" refers to an old English law which stated that a man should beat his wife with a stick no thicker than his thumb.

The abuser is not out of control when he strikes his wife. He is using physical violence in a deliberate way. He chooses who he will batter, what parts of his wife's body he will hit, and when he will abuse (see chapter 6 for a further treatment of the offender).

The Wrong Question: Why Does She Stay?

Why does she stay? This is often the focus when churches and other institutions explore domestic violence. This may appear to be a genuine exploration into understanding the abuse and the victim's response to it. Far too often, however, the attitudes underlying the question can be recognized as a form of blaming the victim. Other statements accompany the question. "If she's staying, she must like it—or at least not be bothered by it." "She must be doing something to cause it."

The question is misdirected. It would be more accurate to ask, "Why is she trapped?" Complex factors work together to keep a wife in an abusive relationship.

What Are the Traps That Keep a Woman in an Abusive Relationship?

The woman is trapped emotionally and in other ways. Financially, she is likely to be dependent on her husband, unable to support herself and the children. She may already have attempted single parenting, and found the stress and isolation of living alone with her children to be unbearable. She wants a father present.

She also struggles with being a faithful Christian. Which is God's will—maintaining her commitment to the permanence of marriage? Or seeking physical safety for herself and her children? Her church community may struggle equally, giving her mixed signals. Recent research indicates that pastors' commitment to the permanence of marriage restricts their ability to counsel women to leave abusive marriages (*Battered into Submission*, pp. 153-154).

Most significantly, she stays because of fear. A woman who leaves an abusive relationship is in danger of receiving even more severe abuse, even to the point of losing her life. The batterer's violence not only controls her behavior in the relationship. It keeps her from leaving the relationship.

Given all these factors, it is remarkable that survivors marshal the resources required to end the relationship. And many women do. In one study, more than 50 percent of survivors were able to get out of violent relationships (*Violence in the Family*, p. 117).

Consequences of Wife Assault

The heartbreaking consequences of physical abuse include the bruises and broken bones and lost lives resulting from physical assaults. Victims also contend with shame, guilt, and, at points, an obliterated sense of worth. An abused woman is burdened with fear and suppressed anger. Her ability to live freely and joyously, to develop and share her gifts, is stifled.

Children and Domestic Violence

A final consequence relates to the way in which family violence affects the children of the home. There is a strong link between domestic violence and child abuse.

One study of more than 900 children at battered women's shelters found that nearly 70 percent of the children were themselves victims of physical abuse or neglect. Five percent had been hospitalized due to the abuse. Most frequently the male batterers had abused the children. In about one-fourth of the cases, both parents abused the children, and in a few instances only the mother.

Children in homes where domestic violence occurs are physically abused or seriously neglected at a rate 1,500 percent higher than in the general population.

Children who grow up in physically abusive homes come to believe that violence is the means to settling conflicts. Many boys grow up repeating the pattern with their wives and children (*Violence in the Family*, p. 113).

The church has a responsibility to recognize the seriousness of these consequences and become active in working toward addressing the injustice of wife abuse.

Wives Abusing Husbands

There are a few situations where wives are the abusers and husbands the victims. These appear to be statistically far less frequent than the abuse of wives by husbands. One study indicates that the abuse of husbands occurs in about 5 percent of reported domestic assaults (*Violence in the Family*, p. 116). Particularly there is a noticeable difference in the severity of injuries between husband abuse and wife abuse. Abused wives receive a far greater number of severe injuries.

There are also cases where men and women assault each other. Most often the wives are acting in self-defense. The wives "lose"; they are the ones who suffer the greatest physical injuries.

Keeping all that in mind, though, it is important to uphold that all physical violence is wrong. The gender of the offender does not make it more or less sin. Men who fear a wife's violence and have been assaulted by her are also victims and need to receive support to break out of the abusive cycles. The abusive wife needs to acknowledge her wrongdoing and seek treatment.

Parents Abusing Children

Returning to the biblical story of Jephthah's sacrifice of his daughter, we noted that it occurred in a particular culture where it was acceptable for parents to kill their children as a religious act. This is an extreme form of parents exercising their physical power over children.

Parents always have greater physical power than their young children. Parents make decisions, based on information they receive from society and the church, about what is an acceptable way to use their superior physical power.

In extreme cases, children suffer broken bones, bruises, or even loss of life. This kind of abuse can and does occur in Christian homes.

To be a faithful community, we need to protect the children in our midst from such abuse. One way we do this is by careful reflection on our own parenting. How do we handle our physical power over our children?

Protestant Churches and Physical Violence Toward Children

We are aided in our discussion by Philip Greven's compelling book *Spare the Child*. Greven traces the thread of physical violence toward children that weaves through North America, particularly but not exclusively, in Protestant churches.

One of the most disturbing themes that Greven develops involves the current Christian literature which endorses physical punishment. Authors such as Larry Christianson, James Dobson, and Larry Tomczak advocate "breaking the child's will." Parents are urged to instill unquestioning obedience in the child at an early age so the child will learn obedience to God. Explicit instructions are given, including the type of instrument to use on the child, the recommendation to strike the child on the buttocks (an area "designed for such a purpose by God"), along with injunctions to continue the punishment until the child submits.

The Consequences of Physical Punishment of Children

Here are some of the consequences of the physical punishment of children Greven describes:

- fear
- anger and hate
- apathy—a lack of empathy
- depression
- rigidity
- dissociation—the splitting of the body from emotional and physical sensations
- sadomasochistic behavior—deriving pleasure from the infliction of physical or mental pain on others or on oneself
- paranoia
- domestic violence
- aggression and delinquency
- authoritarianism: being blindly submissive to authority.

It is difficult to imagine that these are the characteristics God wishes Christian parents to instill in their children.

Greven cites 1 John 4:18, "There is no fear in love. But perfect love casts out fear, for fear has to do with punishment." Fear is incompatible with love.

How can we respond to our children's need for guidance and discipline without using physical punishment? Some of us have no idea, because the use of such punishment is so ingrained in our families and in our culture.

I recognize that this topic is sensitive ground. We have difficulty talking about how we use our physical power with children. In my experience, we bring to these discussions such intense emotions as defensiveness, fear, and guilt. These emotions are related to our experiences as parents who have struck our children, and as children who were struck by our parents.

Today churches and communities across North America hold different standards for the use of physical force with children. As a child, I lived in a community where physical punishment was and is an acceptable means of discipline. As a parent, I live in a community where most adults avoid physical punishment and support each other in developing other forms of discipline.

If we are serious about addressing the violence in our culture, we must move beyond our unwillingness to explore the relationship between abusive parenting and societally acceptable parenting practices that are in fact abusive. We need to explore these interrelationships and to talk with each other about our parenting. We particularly need to find ways to counsel each other in the use of power with our children, noting where we are uncomfortable, and seeking Christian guidance.

We get into difficulty because of our reticence to "pry" into the home. We hesitate to question anyone else's family relationships. We do not want to be nosy. We have our own tensions to negotiate in our relationships with spouses and children. So we parent in isolation rather than sharing our struggles and wisdom.

We all benefit if we develop a willingness to talk openly about our parenting. Some individuals in our church community should know our strengths and weaknesses as parents. This is useful for at least two reasons. Such accountability decreases the likelihood of abuse. And it encourages us to implement healthy, Christ-like parenting strategies.

A growing number of adults are choosing nonviolent approaches to child rearing. Some of these strategies include reasoning; discussion; demonstration of logical consequences; setting of boundaries, rules, and limits; time out and isolation (see Resources for more information on parenting).

As we become more open about our parenting, sharing doubts and stresses as well as strengths, we will create a safer, less violent environment in which to nurture our children.

Elder Abuse

Abuse of the elderly, like the other forms of violence discussed in this book, is not new. In the 1980s, the phenomenon of elder abuse was named and defined. Research began to address it.

It is estimated that four percent of all elderly people are abused; this statistic is believed to be low (from a 1989 Health and Welfare Canada study). Most victims are over seventy-five years of age and female (National Clearinghouse on Family Violence: Health and Welfare Canada).

The abuse can take a number of forms.

• Financial abuse—forcing an older person to sell personal property, stealing an older person's money, pension checks, or possessions; the wrongful use of power of attorney.

• Neglect—abandoning an older person, or withholding food and health services; deliberately failing to give someone what he or she needs.

• Mental abuse—humiliating, insulting, frightening, threatening, or ignoring an older person.

• Physical abuse—slapping, pushing, or beating; sexual assault; forced confinement to a room, bed, or chair.

Usually the abuse is perpetrated by someone who has control or influence over the older person. The abuser may be a family member (spouse or child), a friend, or the staff in a residential facility.

Abusers may be overwhelmed and stressed by—

• the demands of too many people to care for in too short a period of time

• their own ill health (for example, a spouse may have Alzheimer's disease)

• their memories of being abused by the older person they are now caring for.

However, none of these factors excuse mistreatment of the elderly. Elderly people are often reluctant to report the abuse they are experiencing to outside authorities. Most likely they are so dependent on their abuser they have no other options for care and shelter.

We need to recognize this problem and look for alternatives.

We need to acknowledge how our society devalues the elderly, assuming their productivity has diminished with age. We need to encourage the appropriate supports for caregivers, to reduce the likelihood of abuse and neglect. By naming its presence in our midst, we will move toward ending it.

Conclusion

It is disheartening to look squarely into the many faces of physical violence that exist in our most vulnerable and intimate relationships—husband to wife, parent to child, caregiver to elder. Many of us live in fear of attack by strangers, violators who would anonymously mug or beat or rape us. Yet we must recognize that the violence is woven into every layer of our society—on our streets and in our homes, in our schools and work places . . . and in our churches!

To make our communities safe and nurturing, we must recognize and end the violence in our homes.

Prayer

Dear God,

We reel from the burden of physical violence in our church families. We confess that too many of us have supported family violence by our own hands and by turning away from others' troubles.

Cleanse our hearts. Free us from sin. Heal our brokenness. Amen.

Discussion Questions

1. Take time to debrief the emotions that you experienced as you read the chapter. Talk in a safe setting about what you are feeling.

2. In what settings do you use your physical power to control the behavior of others (sports, caregiving)? How do you decide whether your use of force is appropriate or abusive?

3. How did your parents discipline you? How does that affect you today?

4. What messages does the church send about the use of physical force in family relationships? What messages are given

about leadership, control, discipline, obedience?

5. How can the church community encourage people to talk with each other about their family relationships (adult child caring for elderly parent, wife/husband, parent/child) so that we can assist each other in developing empowering relationships?

Resources

Alsdurf, James and Phyllis Alsdurf, *Battered into Submission: The Tragedy of Wife Abuse in the Christian Home*.

Colorosa, Barbara, Video—*Winning At Parenting . . . Without Beating Yours Kids*.

Fortune, Marie M., *Keeping the Faith: Questions and Answers for the Abused Woman*.

Fortune, Marie M., *Violence in the Family*.

Greven, Philip, *Spare the Child: The Religious Roots of Punishment and the Psychological Impact of Physical Abuse*.

Sonkin, Daniel J. and Michael Durphy, *Learning to Live Without Violence*.

Trible, Phyllis, "The Daughter of Jephthah: An Inhuman Sacrifice," *Texts of Terror*.

Weems, Renita J., "A Crying Shame: Jephthah's Daughter and the Mourning Women," *Just a Sister Away*.

3

The Abuse of Sexual Power

Tanya awoke to the familiar sounds of morning in her country home. She smelled the breakfast her mother was preparing, and heard her brother Kurt washing in the bathroom. Then she remembered the cousins who were visiting.

She lay in her bed, naming them. Tim, who at fourteen seemed very old to Tanya's nine years. Betsy, who was eleven and didn't like to play with the same things Tanya did. Six-year-old Buddy, who was mostly a pest. Uncle George, who wasn't really her uncle, but her mother's cousin, a preacher. Aunt Sarah, a quiet woman.

Her door opened. She expected it to be her brother and prepared to yell at him to leave. No. It was Uncle George.

"Good morning," he said, as he smiled and walked over to her bed.

"Hi" she replied. She didn't like that he was moving close.

Uncle George sat down on her bed. Tanya felt uncomfortable. She didn't know what to say. He didn't say anything, just smiled in a weird way. He put his hand on her chest and rubbed her. Then he put his hands under her pajama top! And rubbed her some more.

Tanya's face flamed. She felt like she couldn't move and she felt like she had to move. Why was this grown-up doing this to her?

She pulled away from the hands and turned over. With her chest flat against the bed, she buried her red face in the pillow. Uncle George stood up and walked out of her room.

Tanya was trembling and humiliated. She couldn't imagine telling anyone. The only thing she could think was that she was terribly bad for letting this happen to her.

Introduction

Sexual abuse is a difficult subject; sexual abuse within Christian families is even more difficult for Christians to acknowledge and discuss. It shakes the foundations of our most intimate relationships, our cherished beliefs, and even our identities.

Those of us who have direct experience with sexual abuse know the excruciating pain. Those of us without direct experience often find its existence hard to believe and its devastating effect difficult to comprehend.

Yet the reality of sexual abuse is widespread. According to current estimates, one in three females and one in seven males may be sexually abused by the age of eighteen. One only has to begin to look around to discover survivors—our friends, our family members, our co-workers, ourselves. We will also find offenders in the same groups. Family sexual violence is not a new phenomenon in North American society. What is new is our willingness to address it.

Since the mid-1970s, family sexual abuse has been recognized as a serious problem. Incest survivors have broken the silence to share their stories of sexual abuse. They have developed a number of resources to aid their healing, including books, therapeutic approaches, and support groups. Every institution of society—schools, the criminal justice system, churches, the family—is experiencing the effects of public acknowledgment of child sexual abuse.

Sexual Abuse Between Spouses

We often think of family sexual abuse as that perpetrated by an adult on a child. However, family sexual abuse also occurs between spouses. Most frequently, this involves a husband abusing his wife by making her engage in sexual activities without consent, attacking the sexual parts of her body, or treating her like a sexual object. It is estimated that one in seven wives are victims of marital rape (Diana E. Russell, *Rape in Marriage*).

Sexual violence, like physical and emotional violence, occurs when the offender uses power in ways that harm the victim. Coercion has no place in the sexual activities of Christian couples.

Victims of spousal sexual abuse experience many of the same consequences as incest victims, to whose pain we now turn. I invite you to remember them as you read this chapter.

Definition

The abuse of sexual power occurs in a variety of family settings. In fact, the majority of sexual abuse occurs between people who know each other. If the relationships are not actually family ones—and therefore literally incestuous—they are often family-like.

Victims can be children, teenagers, adults, males, and females. Offenders can be siblings, cousins, grandparents, parents, male and female. Offenders have power over their victims—they are usually older, stronger. Offenders can also be well-respected church members.

The abuse can take a variety of forms. Fondling, kissing, oral sex, vaginal and anal intercourse are examples involving physical contact. The abuse can also take the form of coercion to look at sexually explicit materials or comments about sexual attributes.

The following examples help illustrate.

1. Abigail, twelve, and her brother Nate, thirteen, have been close most of their growing up years. A favorite activity is building a camp in the woods. One night while sleeping out in their newly completed lean-to, Abigail awakens to find Nate's hand sliding into her pants.

2. Three-year-old Joshua's mother comes to his bed fre-

quently. She strokes his penis and moans as she lies beside him.

3. Six-year-old Melinda is brutally raped by her grandfather when he is enraged.

4. Joanne has always known about the stacks of pornographic magazines in her father's shop. Now a teenager, she feels self-conscious and sickened when he comments on women's bodies, especially when he talks about her "figure."

5. Jeff's older brother Mark coerces Jeff into sexual acts with threats of physical violence. Most difficult for Jeff is when Mark forces his penis into Jeff's mouth and ejaculates.

A Bible Story—Amnon's Rape of Tamar

In 2 Samuel 13, we read of King David's daughter Tamar who was sexually abused by her half brother Amnon. Amnon "fell in love" with Tamar, and he "was so tormented that he made himself ill." He consulted his friend and cousin Jonadab who devised a trap for Tamar, which Amnon then set.

Amnon feigned physical illness. When his father King David came to visit him, he asked that his sister Tamar be sent to nurse him. David assented. Tamar came to Amnon's quarters, dressed in the long-sleeved, richly ornamented gown worn by the king's virgin daughters.

At Amnon's request, she made food for him. When the food was ready, he ordered the servants from the room and demanded sexual intercourse. In spite of Tamar's desperate protest, he raped her. Immediately afterward, he hated her and ordered her from his room.

Tamar protested that his sending her away would be a greater wrong than the rape. But Amnon called his servant to remove Tamar and bolted the door. Tamar left, tearing her gown as a sign of her grief, lamenting her loss.

Tamar's brother Absalom avenged the assault on Tamar by killing Amnon two years later. He also took Tamar into his home and named his daughter after her.

Reflections on the Bible Story

In this Bible story, we clearly see the violence and tragedy of family sexual abuse.

1. Amnon is portrayed as cruel and manipulative. He methodically planned his crime. He ignored the cultural and religious prohibitions against such a violent act. Nor did he show any regard for the consequences of his abuse on Tamar.

2. By assaulting Tamar, Amnon asserted his power over her. "Being stronger than she, he forced her." He chose to act in a violent way.

It is vital to uphold a distinction between sexual activity and sexual *violence*. Confusing sexual activity with sexual violence is a problem today as it was in Bible times.

Amnon's assault was sexual violence. Yet the biblical story indicates Amnon "fell in love" with Tamar. Soon this "love" becomes abusive as Amnon "made himself ill because of his sister, for she was a virgin and *it seemed impossible . . . to do anything to her*" (emphasis added).

Tamar herself believed Amnon could have arranged a marriage with her, which would have allowed him to have sexual intercourse with Tamar without the same destructive consequences that resulted from his planned rape. She begged him to delay his demand for intercourse. "Speak to the king, for he will not hold me from you."

Tamar, even as Amnon's wife, would likely have no choice about whether to participate in sexual intercourse. In that regard, the culture perpetuated what I see as sexual violence because Tamar was forced into sexual acts without having a choice.

But if Amnon had married Tamar before forcing himself on her sexually, she would have known a measure of security and status as his wife. Her bargaining can only be seen as a desperate attempt to eke out a tiny shred of self-protection in the face of a violent act that threatened to destroy her.

Amnon, it is clear, does not truly love Tamar. As in other cases of sexual assault, this is a violent act using sexual parts of the body, not a sexual activity (see Marie M. Fortune, *Sexual Violence*, pp. 14-39).

3. Tamar was made more vulnerable to Amnon's assault by the actions of Jonadab and her father, David. Jonadab not only supported Amnon's desire to sexually overpower his half sister, he told Amnon exactly how to set up the circumstances so

Amnon could act out his violence.

David agreed to Amnon's request, which made Tamar more vulnerable. The servants contributed by obeying Amnon's order to leave and then not responding to Tamar's cries.

4. After the assault, King David is described as very angry. It is not clear where his anger is directed. Amnon's sexual abuse of Tamar? The loss of Tamar's economic value to benefit the family? Amnon's endangering his own life by violating his half sister? (Absalom or other male relatives were obliged to protect the females and defend the family honor.)

Whatever the source of his anger, it seems clear David did not act on it. Some biblical texts say, "He would not punish Amnon, because he loved him, for he was his firstborn."

While suggesting David could or should have punished Amnon, these words also indicate David chose to protect Amnon, the offender, rather than respond to the needs of Tamar, the victim.

5. The biblical account offers a vivid picture of the humiliated and lamenting Tamar immediately after the assault. We can guess that Amnon's violation has destroyed Tamar's future as a wife and mother. His forced sexual intercourse means she is not considered virginal. She will no longer be sought as a prized bride and potential mother of children. The last we hear of Tamar is that she remained a desolate woman in her brother Absalom's house.

6. Absalom is the only one we know who came to Tamar's assistance. One can imagine that his offer of shelter to Tamar and her namesake niece were comforts to her. It is not clear that his other actions were helpful. In fact, he initially told her to be quiet and advised her to "not take this to heart."

He killed Amnon as an act of revenge, but we do not know if Amnon's death eased Tamar's pain. Absalom may have killed Amnon because of his hotheadedness (which we know through other Bible stories). Or it may have been his personal need to avenge the wrong done to his family.

Making the Bible Story Our Story

With Amnon's rape of Tamar as background, let us consider

some related dynamics significant today.

1. Like Amnon, sexual abuse perpetrators assert their wants over the needs of their victims. Like Amnon, many offenders manipulate the situation and their victims so they can abuse.

Many incest victims are "groomed" by their offenders so their vulnerability is increased and their ability to defend themselves is decreased. Offenders offer attention and gifts of money or candy. Offenders also appeal to their victim's emotions by appearing helpful or, as in Amnon's case, just the opposite—needing care.

What makes an offender offend? The offender's behavior is a result of a complex mix of factors (which will be considered in more detail in chapter 6). While understanding such factors can guide our response to offenders, it is also important to recognize that each perpetrator is an individual human being who comes to the offenses with a unique history and personality. We need to recognize the limits of our understanding even as we continue to work toward ending family sexual abuse.

2. Power dynamics are a factor in all cases of abuse, as mentioned in other chapters. In our Bible story, Amnon had greater power than Tamar because he was male (and accorded more privilege in his society) and because he was physically stronger.

In matters of sexual abuse, it is important to consider power and resources. Who is older? Who has greater economic resources? Who is responsible for leading the relationship or for maintaining sexual boundaries? Offenders, with the advantage of their greater resources, choose to use their power in sexually abusive ways.

3. As stated before, Tamar had less power than Amnon because she was female. She became increasingly at risk because of Jonadab's treachery and David's agreeing to Amnon's request.

Today the vulnerability of children and the opportunity for molestation can be similar to Tamar's experience, or it can be different. The adults around the child are in a position to assist or inhibit an offender's opportunities.

A child who is left unsupervised is vulnerable to sexual abuse.

A child who does not experience consistent parental love

and affirmation is vulnerable to sexual abuse.

A child hungry for love will sometimes be drawn to an offender's attention, who then sexualizes the relationship.

A child who is not permitted to question adult directives is vulnerable to sexual abuse.

Conversely, a child who is encouraged to set personal boundaries is more protected from sexual abuse.

A child who is educated to respond to unhealthy touch is better equipped to ward off an offender's inappropriate action.

This is not to suggest that all non-offending parents whose children have been sexually abused are responsible for that abuse. The offender is responsible for the abuse. Furthermore, given the power structures of our society, all children are vulnerable to such advances from molesters. Still, adults responsible for a child's protection must consider if they contribute to the child's vulnerability and the opportunity for an offense to occur. And we all must consider how we can make our children less susceptible to sexual abuse.

4. Like Tamar, too often the survivor does not get the support needed for healing. Like Tamar, survivors are told to "forget the past." Or their supporters move to acts of harsh violence that may not be desired by the survivor.

5. The effects of family sexual abuse are severe. We have noted what the Bible tells of the consequences of the rape on Tamar. We can imagine other long-term suffering experienced by Tamar by hearing from survivors today. They indicate that their injuries are similar to people who have experienced a major trauma, such as victims of torture.

Survivors experience intense self-hatred, blocked memories and denial, anger, difficulty trusting others, guilt, and disassociation (splitting off parts of their body experience, numbing, or developing multiple personalities). Obviously a survivor's capacity to experience full and complete enjoyment of sexuality is affected. The sexual abuse damages their ability to enter into the intimate, trusting relationships of spouse and parent.

All of these symptoms make sense given the injury. A survivor feels responsible, partly as a way to gain control of the situation which in reality he could not control. In many cases the survivor was told by the offender that she deserved the abuse or "asked for it." The guilt and the self-hatred result from that misplaced sense of responsibility. Often the self-hatred involves abusing one's body or having a negative body image.

Blocked memories and denial work like pain-numbing drugs. They are a way to minimize the excruciating pain, emotional and in many cases physical, which results from the sexual abuse.

Disassociation is the human body's creative way of self-protecting. When events are too awful to accept, the body "splits" and numbs itself so completely that it does not feel the violations. For example, when Jeff was being abused by his brother, he would focus on the tree outside his bedroom window and pretend he was a twig on a branch. In its most severe form, dissociation involves the creation of separate personalities in the same individual.

While these consequences are common to survivors of sexual abuse, it is important to remember the individuality of the women and men who experience the consequences. It is also helpful to realize that all the consequences develop as the body's unconscious way of taking care of itself when suffering extreme hurt and trauma.

The severity of the injury and the kind of recovery process are affected by a number of factors. These include the relationship between the offender and the survivor, the age of the survivor, the length of time during which the assaults occurred, the intrusiveness of the assaults, and the supports available to the survivor.

Conclusion

Survivors are helped in the long and difficult process of healing when their experiences are listened to and believed and when offenders are held accountable for their actions. (More specifics about recovery are offered in chapter 5.)

Perhaps our efforts are best directed at listening to those directly involved in sexual abuse to learn how to aid the healing of past offenses and to build families, churches, and communities where sexual abuse is no more.

Prayer

Dear God,

We come to the stories of sexual abuse in our church families with many feelings—disbelief, horror, rage, confusion, numbness, fear. Give us listening ears, open hearts, and calm minds to respond with wisdom, compassion, justice, and mercy. Amen.

Discussion Questions

1. Take time to debrief the emotions you experienced as you read the chapter. Talk in a safe setting about what you are feeling.

2. What are you learning about sexual abuse? How do you respond to your learnings? Denial? Anger? (At whom?) Wanting to ignore the topic and hope it goes away? Wanting to work for justice?

3. What information about sexuality were you given as a child? How did that contribute to protecting yourself from sexual abuse or to being vulnerable to sexual abuse?

4. What messages do you hear in church today regarding sexuality and sexual abuse? How does that contribute to healthy sexuality, to sexual abuse?

5. Reflect upon the vulnerable ones in your care. How can you make their world a safer place?

Resources

Brewer, Connie, *Escaping the Shadows, Seeking the Light.*

Fortune, Marie M., *Sexual Violence: The Unmentionable Sin.*

Frank, Jan, *A Door of Hope.*

Heggen, Carolyn Holderread, *Sexual Abuse in Christian Homes and Churches.*

Lew, Michael, *Victims No Longer.*

Trible, Phyllis, "Tamar: The Royal Rape of Wisdom," *Texts of Terror.*

4

The Abuse of
Emotional Power

Linda knew that her friend Hilda was a strict parent. Hilda had been raising her adopted son, David, alone since he was eighteen months old. At that time Hilda's ex-husband had deteriorated mentally. He had always been difficult to live with; then he became threatening and dangerous. Hilda had insisted on a separation.

Hilda often spoke of the loneliness of single parenting, the stress of providing both the income and the nurturing by herself. Linda enjoyed her friendship and tried to help. She wondered if Hilda needed to enforce such exacting standards on the six-year-old boy. Hilda silenced him with a disapproving voice if he expressed sadness or anger. He was not permitted to raise his voice while playing inside the house. His toys always had to be lined up neatly and put away. Hilda sharply curtailed his activities with other children. But Linda kept her questions to herself, not wanting to add to Hilda's burden by criticizing her.

One bright spring day Linda and her husband were visiting Hilda and David, helping with the yard work, planting the vegetable garden, and potting geraniums and impatiens. David was pestering his mother with questions. Linda was shocked when she heard Hilda ask David, "Why don't you go find your mother?"

David seemed confused and mumbled quietly, "You are my mother."

Troubled by Hilda's cruelty, Linda tried to smooth things over. "Of course she's your mother. How about if you and I go play catch?"

Introduction

Emotional abuse. Mental cruelty. These terms relate to violations of a person's emotions or mental state. Let us look more closely at the terms *emotion* and *feelings*.

Emotions give us information about our experiences. Consider the four basic emotions of fear, anger, sadness, and happiness. We experience fear when we feel under attack. Fear, like other emotions, is a message our bodies send to us. Our bodies through fear are saying, "Protect yourself."

Like fear, anger offers a message. Anger signals an injustice or a blocked goal. Sadness informs us of loss. With tears, sighs, and reduced activity, we mourn our losses. When we experience happiness, our smiles, relief, and laughter express our pleasure.

Emotions have a physical counterpart in our bodies, including changes in breathing, heart rate, and sweat gland activity.

We can think of emotions as being similar to the weather—both emotions and weather exist. And the existence of emotions, like the existence of weather, is something we have to come to terms with, like it or not. Like the weather, we have choices about how to respond to our emotions. People vary in terms of their emotional expressiveness, both individually and culturally.

Generally our dominant North American culture does not encourage the expression of the emotions of fear, anger, and sadness. "Don't be a sissy!" a child is scolded for whimpering when a large dog approaches. Anger is suppressed or only given vent in sports contests or violent films. Tears may be viewed as abnormal, inappropriate, or indications of emotional instability.

In our culture, women are often encouraged to express the seemingly "softer" emotions and discouraged from expressing anger. Many men, on the other hand, report that they only know how to recognize and express anger. Some men are so blocked from their emotions they cannot identify their feelings, other than to give vague descriptions like "I get this odd tight sensation" or "There's a kind of rumbling in my chest."

No wonder so much emotional abuse occurs in our families, given our cultural training. We really do not understand our emotions—these rich and valuable expressions of our experiences. Yet we need to learn to identify and express our emotions, because being alienated from our emotions increases the likelihood that emotions will be expressed in inappropriate or abusive ways.

Definition and Examples

Emotional abuse is defined as attacks on one's emotions or mental state, including—

- belittling, humiliating
- name calling
- threatening to abandon or give a child away
- attacking a person's self-esteem
- lying or manipulating the person's sense of reality.
- neglect—failure to provide food, clothing, shelter, medical care, or adequate supervision.

Emotional abuse can occur by itself. Parents can damage their child emotionally by regularly attacking the child's self esteem. This hurts even if the parent never lays a forceful hand on the child or never violates the child sexually. However, physical abuse and sexual abuse always include emotional abuse.

The child who is being sexually abused experiences fear among other emotions. She is unable to protect herself or have someone to listen to her fears. She is damaged emotionally.

The child who is being physically abused will experience anger, among other feelings. Yet he cannot express his anger directly to his abuser, because he will receive more physical abuse. His ability to express his anger in appropriate ways is damaged.

A Bible Story—Sarah's Abuse of Hagar

The biblical story we explore in this chapter involves emotional abuse. We could also say it involves physical abuse, although that is not the concern of Genesis 16:1-15 and 21:8-21. (I am indebted to Phyllis Trible for her critique of this passage in *Texts of Terror*, pp. 9-35.)

Hagar was the Egyptian slave-girl of Sarah, Abraham's wife. Sarah was infertile, so she said to Abraham, "You see that the Lord has prevented me from bearing children; go in to my slave-girl; it may be that I shall obtain children by her." Abraham agreed and conceived a child with Hagar.

When Hagar knew she was pregnant, she looked with contempt on her mistress. Sarah appealed to Abraham, "May the wrong done to me be on you! I gave my slave-girl to your embrace, and when she saw that she had conceived, she looked on me with contempt. May the Lord judge between you and me!"

Abraham quickly sidestepped his responsibility for Hagar and their unborn child. "Your slave-girl is in your power; do to her as you please." Then Sarah dealt harshly with Hagar (probably beat her) so Hagar fled from Sarah.

An angel of God came to Hagar near a spring in the desert and told her, "Return to your mistress, and submit to her." The angel also said, "I [God] will so greatly multiply your offspring that they will be too numerous to count," and made additional prophecies about her child.

Hagar returned to Sarah and Abraham and birthed a son, Ishmael. Fourteen years later Sarah conceived and had a son, Isaac.

At the feast marking Isaac's weaning, Sarah saw Ishmael playing and commanded Abraham, "Cast out this slave woman with her son, for the son of this slave woman shall not inherit along with my son Isaac."

The matter was very distressing to Abraham on account of his son. But God said, "Do not be distressed because of the boy and . . . your slave woman; whatever Sarah says to you, do as she tells you, for it is through Isaac that offspring shall be named for you. As for the son of the slave woman, I will make a nation of him also, because he is your offspring."

Early the next morning, Abraham took some bread and a skin of water and gave them to Hagar and sent her off with the boy. She wandered into the desert.

When the water was gone, she cast the child under one of the bushes and moved a short distance away, saying, "Do not let me look on the death of the child."

God heard the voice of the boy, and the angel of God called to Hagar from heaven, saying, "What troubles you, Hagar? Do not be afraid; for God has heard the voice of the boy where he is. Come, lift up the boy and hold him fast with your hand, for I will make a great nation of him." Then God opened Hagar's eyes and she saw a well of water. So she went and filled the skin with water and gave the boy a drink.

God was with the boy, and he grew up, an archer who lived in the desert. His mother "got a wife for him" from Egypt.

Reflections on the Bible Story

1. The text could be read as suggesting Hagar started the fight. Hagar looked with contempt on her mistress, Sarah, when she knew she was pregnant. Does her behavior justify the cruelty Hagar and Ishmael received from Sarah and Abraham?

2. Sarah mistreated Hagar; Hagar fled in response to this mistreatment. The mistreatment likely took the form of physical abuse—beatings, slapping, etc.

3. Sarah took no responsibility for her role in the strife, blaming Abraham for the tension she experienced with Hagar's pregnancy.

4. Sarah denied Ishmael his rightful share of the inheritance, insisting that Isaac be the only heir.

5. Though Abraham was distressed, he did not protect Hagar or Ishmael and even personally exiled them into the desert. Depriving family members of shelter and food is neglect and abuse.

6. The presence of God (the angel) was comforting at some points and at other points disturbing. God saved Hagar and Ishmael by revealing a water source, and God repeatedly promised that Ishmael would have many descendants.

Yet God also appeared to side with the powerful against the oppressed. God's angel told Hagar to submit to her mistress.

Can this mean to submit to the beatings from Sarah? Surely the angel knew the abusive situation to which Hagar was returning. When Abraham was distressed about his son, God referred to Ishmael as "the boy" and told Abraham not to be distressed. How can we interpret this message from God when Hagar and Ishmael were clearly at risk of losing their lives by being sent from the security of Abraham's tents into the harshness of the desert?

Making the Bible Story Our Story

1. Conflict exists within families. Sometimes family members do not even like each other. That seems to be the case with Hagar and Sarah. They first were bound together as mistress and slave. Sarah drew the bonds tighter in her desperate response to her infertility. As mothers of sons of the same father, their tension was inflamed, leading Sarah to hatred and vengeful acts.

2. The side players in a conflict can increase or decrease the abuse. Abraham was in a position to play a mediating influence, yet he seemed to do little more than assist Sarah in implementing her abuse.

3. The abuse does not go away. In this family's story, the abuse continued and increased until Hagar and Ishmael were forced out of the family. Tragically the struggle between the descendants of these two brothers, both sons of Abraham, continues in the lives of Israelites and Palestinians today.

4. Sometimes victims of abuse have no real choices. Perhaps the angel of God sent Hagar back into the oppressive situation because it afforded the best place for her to raise an infant. Surely she would have struggled against insurmountable odds to care for herself and a baby in the desert. When she was permanently banished, Ishmael was a teenager and able to contribute to her care as well as his.

5. It is often the power imbalance that sets up the abuse. Because Sarah was Hagar's mistress, she had the power to beat and banish her, with her child. Hagar gained status as Abraham's wife and the mother of his son, but only temporarily. Hagar's contempt of Sarah may have been rooted in the injustices of the power imbalance.

Naming Emotional Abuse

With whom do you identify in this Bible story? Are you sympathetic to the abused Hagar or the rejected son Ishmael? Are you drawn to the perplexed Abraham or the furious Sarah?

Wherever our initial sympathies lie, it is important to recognize the line between good and evil and to declare ourselves in partnership with good and in resistance to evil. In this story, Hagar may have been difficult to live with and Ishmael a painful reminder of Sarah's lengthy infertility. At the same time, Sarah and Abraham abused their power as mistress, husband, and father by rejecting and banishing Hagar and Ishmael.

Emotional abuse is often more difficult to recognize than physical or sexual abuse. Because it affects emotions, it is less tangible than physical assaults or sexual violations. Yet it is just as real, just as deadly.

Emotional abuse can be conveyed by the spoken word. It can also be indicated by silence—a cold, blaming silence or the silence of not listening. Or it can be a calculating, devastating, nonverbal expression that says without words, "I hate you. You're awful."

I often heard a family friend comment in the presence of her children, "My children are so plain. They aren't at all pretty." Such remarks violate a child's spirit as surely as a physical slap.

We all learned the rhyme "Sticks and stones will break my bones but words will never hurt me." This verse undoubtedly shielded us against schoolyard taunts, or helped us endure the teasing of our siblings. But the rhyme is not true. Words do hurt.

Imagine being the target of these comments:

"You are the most ungrateful child I ever knew."

"You have the devil in you!"

"That does it! I'm calling Children's Aid to place you in a foster home."

The Effects of Emotional Abuse

Emotional abuse obviously damages the survivor's self-esteem. It is difficult to maintain self-confidence and self-worth in the face of repeated belittling and attacking comments.

The effects of other kinds of abuse are felt by emotional

abuse survivors. Effects include fear, depression, inability to trust, and difficulty being comfortable in social situations. Some survivors model themselves after their offenders and become abusive toward others.

Power Dynamics

As in other abusive situations, it is important to consider the power and resources of the individuals. Offenders have greater resources than victims. Offenders use their power to control and intimidate their victims. Keep this in mind as we consider emotional abuse between adults and children and between adults.

Adult-Child Abuse

In adult-child relationships, the adult has power over the child. There is truth to the joke that an infant in the house is an example of minority rule. Even so the infant is desperately dependent on the adults for life itself. Among other resources, adults have greater physical, emotional, and economic power than children.

We often do not recognize the tremendous power adults hold over children. The following anecdote offers a glimpse of how children perceive adult's power.

A mother dutifully determined it was time to introduce her child to the great body of literature called fairy tales. With some trepidation about the effect of the gruesome violence, she began with "Jack and the Beanstalk." Snuggling her son under her arm, she read the story.

When she finished, he immediately queried, "There aren't really giants, are there, Mommy?"

Before she could reply reassuringly, he answered himself, "There *are* adults."

Adults are the giants in children's fairy tales. The recurring themes of fear, danger, catastrophe, and violence of those age-old tales likely reflect the experiences of the children at the hands of the giant adults.

Adults need to remain conscious of that fact. When children are so dependent on us for their physical, emotional, and spiritual well-being, our words and our actions are larger than life. We have enormous potential to shape the child for good or evil.

The Generations Repeat

Our involvement with children (as parents or other care-givers) is tempered by our own childhood experiences.

Our responses to children are affected by the joyful and the traumatic events we knew as children. For example, we are greatly influenced by the parent models we knew.

I heard many throwaway lines from my parents as they were raising us. I call them throwaway lines because I "threw them away." These comments were made in sheer frustration, cannot be responded to, and are best shed, like water off a duck's back (if one is able).

Here are some throwaway lines I remember:

"I can't keep anything nice around you kids."

"Go ahead and do what you want. You always do anyhow."

"I hope you have six kids just like yourself."

I vowed I would avoid such unpleasant and unproductive communication. I labored to make my parenting messages clear and reasonable.

"Mama is sad when you break her earring" (this said to a pre-schooler).

"You may not play ball hockey on the street. It's not safe. We need to come up with another alternative."

"I get frustrated when you speak rudely to me."

Imagine my astonishment when my son exploded one day, "How many times do I have to tell you?" The rest of his tirade was lost as I experienced the sensation of time traveling back thirty years as my son became my parent and I, just as swiftly, was transformed from mother to child.

I checked it out later with my husband, noting my surprise. "You say it all the time," he answered ruefully.

Breaking family patterns is hard work.

Adult-Adult Abuse

Emotional abuse can and does occur in adult relationship. Adults, male and female, are capable of humiliating another adult or attacking another adult's self esteem. Attacks can some-times be disguised as jokes, often (though not always) by males at the expense of females.

A Word to All

In James 3, we read of the dangers of the tongue. Verse 9 can be readily paraphrased, "With the tongue we both praise God and curse our loved ones, who have been made in God's like-ness. My brothers and sisters, that should not be."

Our words, our gestures, our silences—all have the power to injure. Many adults will find themselves guilty of one or more forms of emotional abuse. It is valuable to recognize ourselves as powerful people, with the ability to build or destroy the self-worth of others.

At a low point in my life and my marriage, I recall raging at my spouse as I drove us to an appointment. We were running late, which set off my explosion. But not the fact that we were late, nor my spouse, nor even my emotional exhaustion was re-sponsible for the abusive manner in which I expressed my anger that day. I bear the responsibility for mismanaging my frustra-tion.

Following the incident, I took steps to prevent such an ex-treme incident from reoccurring. I worked to balance my life so I experienced less emotional overload. I sought to deal with stresses as they arose rather than allowing them to accumulate, then dumping my frustration where it does not belong. Having heard from my husband (and my child) that my loud, intense ex-pression of anger is difficult (even frightening) for them, I at-tempted quieter, more contained statements of anger.

As we consider abuse in Christian families, we need to keep in mind human ability to choose between good and evil. The line between good and evil does not separate human beings into two groups of good and bad people. Rather the line cuts down through every human heart. We all face the choice between good and evil and must live with the consequences of our choices.

Conclusion

Much emotional abuse arises from an unwillingness to step into the shoes of the other. We fail to recognize how confusing and frightening the world of adults is to children. We project onto our spouse the leftover wounds of our childhood, venting on them the anger and pain that relates directly to experiences we had with our first family members.

As adults we must recognize the wounds of our inner child and work toward healing (see chapters 1 and 6). We must find ways to heal from the conflicts with our parents, so we do not perpetuate the sins of our fathers and mothers.

We must build empowering relationships. We must speak to our intimates in mutually respectful ways. When dealing with children, we must put ourselves into their perspectives and address them with respect and dignity. We also must take responsibility for our wrongdoings.

Prayer

Dear God,

You know us in our inmost beings. Our emotions are as precious to you as are our physical characteristics. You desire wholeness for us emotionally as well as physically and spiritually. You know our emotions can be nurtured or abused. You witness us as we nurture and abuse other's emotions.

Call us to accountability. Restore us to health. Amen.

Discussion Questions

1. Take time to discuss the emotions you experienced as you read the chapter. In a safe setting, share your feelings.

2. How were emotions valued or devalued in your first family? How does that affect you today?

3. Do you recall any "throw away" lines from your parents? (page 61) In what settings are you likely to use such lines today?

4. What emotional abuses are you prone to (cold silences, sarcasm, "looks that kill")? What have you found to be helpful in curbing such abuse?

5. What emotional abuses do you observe as a friend or family member? Brainstorm as a group how you might respond to such abuses.

Resources

Trible, Phyllis, "Hagar: The Desolation of Rejection," *Texts of Terror.*

Weems, Renita, "A Mistress, A Maid, and No Mercy: Hagar and Sarah," *Just a Sister Away.*

5
The Healing Path
for Survivors

MEG TRUSTED A. J., her pastor. He was one of the few people she trusted. She had been more vulnerable with him than with anyone. Yet she struggled with his current directive, "Go for counseling."

Meg protested. She carried painful memories from previous experiences with counselors. One therapist denounced her as "the most manipulative woman" he had ever seen. Her former pastor had suggested they meet alone at his office late in the evening. She refused, and called the bishop's office to report her pastor for behaving inappropriately. She did not trust counselors.

A. J. insisted. He recommended a nearby Christian agency. Reluctantly Meg decided to give counseling one more try. She dialed the agency's number and arranged an appointment with the secretary. When she hung up the phone, she knew that her new counselor was female. Meg noted two feelings: great fear and a little relief.

At the first session, Meg met a woman about her own age.

Meg told her story, speaking rapidly and honestly. She was separated from her husband, Terrance. The children were living with her and visited their father frequently.

Meg chose her words carefully as she described her marriage as "difficult." She described her ex-husband as moody and spoke of his emotional abuse.

She was quick to note how she had participated in her marriage's breakdown. Meg was a dedicated youth worker. She had met and been drawn to a co-worker, Sean. They had an affair. Her youngest child was conceived during that affair.

Still she had tried to seek help for her marriage, as had Sean, who was also married. She attended counseling with Terrance, only to feel violated in the counseling. The counselor insisted she was to blame, and that she needed to do all the changing. She was never able to discuss Terrance's frequent verbal and occasional physical abuse, because the counselor viewed these comments as her "passing the buck."

Sean too had been unable to reconcile his marriage and had separated from his wife.

Meg finally insisted that Terrance leave. "We cannot live this way," she declared.

Terrance left, but not without a violent sexual assault.

"He doesn't see it as rape," she told the counselor. "He says he was just asserting his rights as a husband."

"It's rape," the counselor responded. "Forced sex is rape."

The first session passed swiftly. Meg continued to meet regularly with the counselor and learned to trust her. The counseling office became a refuge for Meg, a place of safety and nurture.

Over time Meg recounted Terrance's abuse. She realized he had often been sexually abusive as well as physically and emotionally violent. As she explored the sexual violations, she recalled, with stunning force, childhood sexual abuse by her grandfather. She also unpacked the many layers of her troubled relationship with her mother.

Outside the sessions, Meg continued to parent her children in nurturing ways. After much soul-searching and pastoral care, she and Sean married. She attempted to set limits with Terrance, who remained frighteningly invasive. She returned to youth ministry and found herself in demand as a resource person for youth events and women's retreats. Meg chose not to publicly identify herself as a survivor. Yet her pastoral leadership was powerfully marked by her own experience. In a pit of overwhelming despair and terror, Meg sought for and found a faithful, loving God. Her healing is ongoing.

Introduction

What is the healing process for a survivor of family violence? What makes a victim a survivor? What inner resources are required? What supports are needed? How long does it take?

Each person is a unique human being. Each survivor has a unique healing path. While common themes can be found, each person must "walk the lonesome journey" alone. Words do not adequately convey the experience. Survivors assure me that the process of healing is not neat or tidy or ever finished.

Themes we will consider in this chapter include building supports, trusting the inner guide, naming the abuse, remembering the abuse, anger, grieving, confrontation, justice-making, spiritual resources, and living with the abuse.

Building Supports

Each survivor will walk an individual path of healing. At some points that feels indescribably lonely. Perhaps it can be compared to our faith journeys, which each of us attends to with "fear and trembling." Even so we are sustained and enriched on our faith journeys by traveling companions.

The same is true for survivors. Each survivor benefits from developing a network of supportive people. Other survivors can be particularly understanding and helpful; survivor groups are valuable. Sometimes family members are able to support and nurture. Other times family members contribute to the problem, past and present.

Some survivors turn to counselors for guidance. Other survivors do not use professional counselors but work at their healing in self-help groups or in other ways. Some survivors find trusted friends in church. Some are helped by a pastor.

Many survivors find it difficult to be vulnerable enough to

trust others. When a boy is brutally violated as a child, he will be frightened that another human being will hurt him again. His self-protection forms armor around his tender wounds. It is difficult for him to risk.

Still each survivor needs to have a network of people who will offer compassion and loving presence as the survivor heals. Building that network is one of the major tasks of recovery.

Trusting the Inner Guide

Each survivor learns to trust the inner guide. God speaks to each of us, guiding us in making wise choices.

When Jade was most distressed, in the early stages of recalling childhood sexual abuse, she experienced an inner voice instructing her to work in her garden. Whenever the panic threatened to overwhelm her, Jade would don work clothes and go out to her backyard. The warmth of the sun, the chirp of the birds, the wriggle of a fat earthworm, the rhythm of pulling weeds—all these things nurtured her into calmness.

Raymond discovered that journaling was a useful tool in claiming his inner voice. He carried a notebook and pen with him at all times. When he was confused or enraged or depressed, he began to write his feelings and the events he was experiencing. The journaling helped him focus and gain direction.

Trusting one's instincts is particularly important to survivors because of the damage they have received. Abuse is not normal; our bodies and spirits cry out against such violation. Yet many survivors experience abuse over and over again.

One's inner sense of what is right and wrong, healthy and unhealthy, gets distorted. During the abuse, the more powerful offender overrode the survivor's instinct for self-protection. Reclaiming the inner guide is a key to health.

As survivors claim their inner wisdom, they grow stronger and clearer in the knowledge of what is necessary for recovery.

Naming the Abuse

"You will know the truth, and the truth will make you free." Jesus' words from John 8:32 have a particular significance to the survivor of domestic violence.

Much of the abuse has occurred under conditions of lies, secrecy, and false appearances. Naming the abuse has the effect on those lies that a candle has in illuminating the darkness of a deeply buried cave. It dispels deception.

It is difficult to name the abuse for at least two reasons. First, in many cases the offender has deliberately blocked truth-telling.

"If you tell Mommy what has happened, she will leave us and you'll never see her again."

"You were a bad boy. You deserved it."

"No one else remembers it the way you do."

Counseling is so effective in the healing process in part because counselors *listen*. The abused person can speak the truth without judgment or reprisals. A survivor spared the obligation of defending is in a better position to explore and remember. Survivors move into a greater position of strength by having their experiences given attention, much the way a caring nurse gently tends a physical wound.

Second, the trauma of the abuse is often so great that the survivor has literally forgotten it. That is, the survivor's protective denial mechanism has blocked the memory from consciousness in order to spare the individual more trauma.

This blocking is effective in the short term but is maintained at great expense. For underneath the block is a frightened, terrorized child. The child huddles for protection until safety is realized.

Much of the literature on childhood sexual abuse suggests survivors remember the assaults only when they are "ready." Still the trauma of the wall crumbling, and the full force of those memories impacting, is often an overwhelming onslaught.

Remembering the Abuse

Ruth Krall, who studied rape for her doctoral dissertation, describes rape as "dis-membering" the victim. The brutality of rape is so great that it psychologically strips a person of her parts—her sense of safety, her personal boundaries, her ability to sleep. Healing is a process of "re-membering," putting the parts back together.

This vivid metaphor can be employed for other survivors of domestic violence. The remembering is a means of reclaiming lost parts. The healing journey is aimed at experiencing life as a whole person, with all of one's parts intact.

Remembering, even though it is a necessary part of the healing, is excruciating. One survivor of physical abuse describes her experience this way:

> A beating is a hard thing to describe. It's a hard thing to remember, not because the memories have faded, but because they are so clear and painful. I felt an indescribable fear, my arms pinned immobile to a bed by the knees of the man I loved, his fist coming toward my face. (From the September 1987 *Women's Concerns Report*, a publication of Mennonite Central Committee.)

For the survivor in the early stages of recovery, the remembering is so difficult because it feels exactly as if it is happening all over again. The body has registered physical memories of the violations. As the mind recalls the experiences, the body recalls the physical sensations. This is an extremely frightening and draining time for the survivor. Basic nurturing supports are often required, such as a mug of hot chocolate, soft blankets, or cuddly teddy bears.

Some survivors have a great need to talk and will do so in many times and places, playing the mental video of abuse over again and again. Some survivors become silent, not finding words adequate to describe their pain. Others express their memories and feelings by writing in a journal or by creating art—music, poetry, or drawings.

The abuse incidents pull like a powerful underwater current. Each time the survivor is immersed in the memory, it threatens to engulf him. He does survive, though.

With time, he notices that he has survived, that the memories no longer totally engulf him, that he can recall an incident without having the same overwhelming terror. The abuse has moved from being experienced as if it were occurring again to a *memory*, an event that happened in the past. As a memory, it no longer has the power to overtake the survivor completely.

Anger

Anger is a healthy, God-given response to injustice. Given the extent of the violation, we need not be surprised by the fury a survivor may express. Yet we may be ill-prepared to deal with it. As one criminal justice official declared, "I could handle these battered wives better if they weren't so angry."

In the Christian church we are likely to give and receive messages that suppress anger. We are keenly uncomfortable with it. Understandably so. Most of our experiences with anger have been destructive. People have gotten scorched by it. Yet anger can offer empowering energy when constructively channeled.

Another difficulty is our mistaken belief that one cannot be angry *and* loving. We need to recognize that anger is a normal human response in many relationships—including loving, intimate ones. As we become more accepting of our own and other's anger, we are more able to assist in the healing of survivors. Survivors need people who accept their anger as a valid response to the violations they have suffered.

In our anger expressions, it is necessary to avoid physically hurting ourselves or others. Alcohol and drug abuse are not effective means of managing anger. Anger is managed more effectively if directed to its target rather than being "dumped" where it does not belong.

People have found the following to be useful, constructive expressions for anger:

- punching pillows
- screaming in a solitary place
- writing a letter to the offender which may or may not be sent
- role-playing—having an imaginary conversation with the offender
- physical exercise—walking, rug-weaving, gardening, racquet sports.

All of us—survivors, offenders, and witnesses—need to attend to the task of responsible anger management.

Grieving

Grieving is that part of the healing process where the survivor mourns the losses. Family violence destroys; many of the losses are permanent.

Taso did not experience the nurturing protection a child deserved from his father; that part of his childhood is lost forever. Elena was committed as a Christian to her marriage being permanent. Leaving her abusive husband meant the loss of that ideal, along with a number of other losses.

There is no quick fix for grieving. Poetry, music, and art are often the best companions during times of mourning. The friend who offers a hand to hold or a hug, or who sits alongside silently, or weeps in solidarity—that friend is a gem.

Grief cannot be hurried. Survivors (and their supporters) can become impatient, but grief cannot be pushed. It takes whatever time it takes.

Confrontation

Placing the blame on the offender is another necessary part of the healing. Those survivors who were abused as children affirm that they are not responsible for the suffering and behaviors of their abusers. Those who were victimized as adults take responsibility for their actions while at the same time placing the responsibility for the abuse on the offender.

Some survivors find value in direct confrontations. They plan carefully to choose a time and setting that seems right. They may have supporters present. Speaking directly to the offender or by sending a letter, they name the abuse, describe its effect on them, and often instruct the offender to seek treatment to. end the abusive behaviors.

Some survivors are led to such confrontations by Jesus' teaching in Matthew 18 on church discipline. In this passage, people (survivors) are encouraged to openly name the abuse to the offender. These instructions contrast with comments like "It happened so long ago. Just forget it." Or "Christians should suffer silently" (a further treatment of Matthew 18 can be found in chapter 8).

In some cases, survivors and offenders discover healing and hope through such encounters. This is most likely to happen when offenders acknowledge their wrongdoing, express remorse, and agree to change.

However, most of the time offenders deny any violation or slide from assuming responsibility.

"If I mistreated you, it's because my father mistreated me."

"I never hit you. I just slapped you once or twice."

"You liked it as much as I did. You know you did."

Survivors must prepare carefully for such a response, thinking through in advance of the confrontation, "What is my goal?" If the goal is to have the offender take full responsibility for the offense, the survivor may be severely disappointed. The survivor's healing cannot be dependent on the offender's willingness to take ownership, although healing can certainly be encouraged by the offender's acknowledgment of guilt. Many survivors set as a goal that they are placing the responsibility for the abuse in the offender's hands. Such a goal empowers them by maintaining personal control over the success of reaching the goal.

Other survivors go a less direct, but potentially as effective, route.

Gina placed her confronting note in her grandfather's hand as he lay in his casket. Jose confronted his older brother during a role-play in his counselor's office. Michelle confronted her mother at her mother's grave. Gina, Jose, and Michelle all experienced relief and were able to move on in their healing even without direct contact with their offender.

Many survivors require a "time-out" from their offenders. They choose to carefully limit the time when they are together. This is a necessary part of the healing. Christians may have difficulty accepting the need for such limits by the survivor. This challenges deeply held beliefs about the permanence of family bonds. All of us must recognize that it is the abuse which destroyed the family ties.

It is true that everyone, especially the survivor, suffers when the survivor finds it necessary to sever family relationships. One survivor describes himself as an orphan because of his parents' abuse and the breakdown in relationships. Witnesses can offer to be substitute family members.

The survivor's act of self-preservation needs to be supported. Consider these words from 1 Corinthians 3:16-17: "Do you not know that you are God's temple and that God's Spirit dwells in you? If anyone destroys God's temple, God will destroy that person. For God's temple is holy, and you are that temple." Here we are given a mandate that we must care for our physical bodies because they are the temple of God. Survivors will benefit if witnesses encourage them to care for themselves.

Justice-Making

Survivors, as they heal, require experiences of justice. The abuse they suffered was unjust. To heal they must experience justice. The church community can become an important part of the justice-making in family violence.

Survivors heal when the church supports and empowers them (see chapter 10). Some survivors turn to the courts as a means of seeking justice. They launch civil suits as a means of holding the offender accountable. By taking such action, many survivors want the offender to accept responsibility for his offense.

Unfortunately the adversary nature of our legal system reduces the likelihood of that happening. Many offenders plead not guilty and spend great effort defending themselves.

Some survivors do receive financial awards as a result of launching their suits. This money is significant, in part because it assists the survivor with the financial cost of recovery (counseling, loss of work). It is also restitution, something given by the offender (even if court-mandated) to acknowledge responsibility for the survivor's suffering.

The survivor, as she heals, is addressing the power issues that related to the abuse. Her healing includes recognizing and using her power. By so doing, she changes the power dynamics between her and her offender. Previously the offender had used his power to harm her. In healing, the survivor uses her power (for example, to choose when and if she will see the offender, to confront the abuser, to sue the offender) to care for herself. This action "breaks the spell" of the past, when the offender had power over her.

Spiritual Resources

> But now thus says the Lord,
> he who created you, O Jacob,
> he who formed you, O Israel:
>> Do not fear,
> for I have redeemed you;
>> I have called you by name, you are mine.
>> When you pass through the waters,
> I will be with you;
>> and through the rivers,
> they shall not overwhelm you;
>> when you walk through fire
> you shall not be burned,
>> and the flame shall not consume you.
>> (Isaiah 43:1-2)

Finding spiritual resources is another part of the healing. Many survivors turn to the church and Christianity for support. Some find comfort in verses such as the Isaiah passage. Some find church leaders who understand and support their healing. Some survivors create new art to express their experiences.

Consider this poem written by an anonymous survivor of incest as she reflected on the statue of a crucified woman. (This statue by Almuth Lutkenhaus hangs at Emmanuel College in Toronto, Ontario.)

> O God, through the image of a woman
> crucified on the cross
> I understand at last.

> For over half my life
> I have been ashamed
> of the scars I bear.
> These scars tell an ugly story,
> a common story,
> about a girl who is a victim
> when a man acts out his fantasies.

> In the warmth, peace, and sunlight of your presence
> I was able to uncurl the tightly clenched fists.
> For the first time
> I felt your suffering presence with

me in that event.
I have known you as a vulnerable
baby, as a brother, and as a father.
Now I know you as a woman.
You were there with me
as the violated girl
caught in helpless suffering.

The chains of shame and fear
no longer bind my heart and body.
A slow fire of compassion and forgiveness is kindled.
My tears fall now
for man as well as woman.

You, God, can make our violated bodies
vessels of love and comfort
to such a desperate man.
I am honored to carry this womanly power
within my body and soul.

You were not ashamed of your wounds.
You showed them to Thomas
as marks of your ordeal and death.
I will no longer hide these wounds of mine.
I will bear them gracefully.
They tell a resurrection story.

Many survivors struggle painfully in their attempts to forge connections with the church and Christianity. The abuse itself may have been linked with Christian symbols. One survivor was forced to read Bible verses before she was raped.

Passages such as the one from Isaiah seem hollow and mocking for survivors who did not experience God when they were being abused. In a typical morning worship service, there are too many triggers which remind them of the trauma of their abuse. They may experience church as full of "oughts and shoulds," which reminds them of the "oughts and shoulds" connected with abuse. Their experience with family violence is not addressed in honest, helpful ways. Many survivors leave the church, sometimes temporarily, sometimes permanently, seeking for places where they are nurtured spiritually.

Women who have been abused by men are often troubled by

images of God which are exclusively male. Some survivors turn to other images (God as Spirit, God as Comforter, God as Mother) to express their faith. The following song by Miriam Therese Winter is typical of such offerings.

Mother and God,
To you we sing.
Wide is your womb,
Warm is your wing.
In you we live,
Move and are fed
Sweet flowing milk,
Life giving bread.
Mother and God,
To you we bring
All broken hearts,
All broken wings.

(Words and music by Sister Miriam Therese Winter, copyright © 1987 by Medical Mission Sisters. Used by permission)

Many survivors offer the gift of their remarkable faith journey to the church. Out of the desert of their cruel experiences, they are leading the church into new, deeper understandings of God, faith, and healing. They bear powerful testimony to God's redeeming presence. Witnesses can listen to and learn from them, and give thanks.

Living with the Abuse

Our life experiences stay with us. The tender and the disturbing remain engraved in our memories, physically and mentally, for as long as we live. The wonderfully comforting sensation of being snuggled against my father's broad chest is as much a part of me as the stinging pain of his hand angrily spanking my buttocks.

The survivor needs to find a way to live with the abuse. Many survivors struggle with the continued effect the abuse has on their lives.

"I wouldn't need to be here in counseling if not for him."

"This hurts too much. I want it to go away."

"I can't enjoy sex because of the abuse."

At some point, though, the survivor can state, "This happened. I can't change what is in the past. I can focus on the present and how I want my life to be today."

When that moment came for Ali, she declared, "I've always been waiting for things to happen to me. I've been stymied by the abuse. Now I'm going to follow my dreams."

One Christian writer speaks of "making a shelter for my sorrow in my heart." This is the process of living with the abuse. The abuse has a place in one's life. It is not all of one's life. It is not removed from one's life.

The survivor creates a shelter, a room if you like, in one part of her heart. There the memory of the abuse resides. She visits it on occasion, sometimes by choice, sometimes involuntarily. But it is a contained memory, and no longer overwhelms.

Prayer

Dear God,

You are the Source of our being. We know you created us in tender compassion and desire us to live in wholeness. We bring our brokenness to you and trust your tender mercies will heal us. Amen.

Discussion Questions

1. What do you have to offer survivors as they heal?

2. How do you respond when survivors express anger?

3. What have you learned that is helpful for your own inner healing as you walk alongside family violence survivors?

4. What resources does your congregation have to assist survivors? What resources would you like to develop?

Resources

See Chapter 3 Resources

Davis, Laura, *Allies in Healing.*

Evert, Kathy and Inie Bijkerk, *When You're Ready: A Woman's Healing from Childhood Physical and Sexual Abuse by Her Mother.*

Keen, Jane A., *A Winter's Song: A Liturgy for Women Seeking Healing from Childhood Sexual Abuse.*

Wisechild, Louise M., ed., *She Who Was Lost Is Remembered: Healing from Incest Through Creativity.*

6
Offenders

I GLIMPSED GEORGE as I walked into the waiting room. With his back turned to me, I registered fleeting impressions—middle-aged, medium build, Caucasian, nothing striking.

I introduced myself, outstretching my hand. He shook it briefly and I noted other characteristics—his face had pleasant wrinkles, his curly hair was receding. He smiled and spoke so swiftly that his words were pushed together. I had an initial sense of liking this man, which always helps counseling begin positively.

Once we were settled in my office, I completed an intake form recording data such as address and marital and educational status. George responded directly to all my questions, with that same rapid speech. Making eye contact, I noted George's striking deep-brown eyes, which were simultaneously intense and guarded. I finally opened the counseling formally by inquiring, "What is it that brings you here?"

George spoke even more quickly, revealing his nervousness. "I have violent fantasies. I imagine hurting women—raping them. Then I sexually molested my daughter, and I realize I'm really out of control on this."

By the end of the interview, I learned that George had never acted on his violent fantasies, that he had turned himself in for his inappropriate sexual behavior with his daughter, that he had been convicted and sentenced, and that he was participating regularly in a sex offender's group. He was most devastated by the loss of regular contact with his children.

He spoke briefly of his own childhood, which was marked by vicious beatings by his father.

George then turned his brown eyes on me and said, "So, how are you with this? Can you handle it?"

* * * * * * * * * *

Introduction

Sex offender. Wife beater. Child molester. Abusive parent.

How do you respond to such terms? What emotional reactions do you have? Chances are you experience fear and revulsion. It is difficult to remember the person behind the label. In many ways our responses to offenders are different from our responses to survivors. Many times witnesses who have opened their hearts to listening to a survivor's experience naturally identify with the survivor in raging at injustice.

It is often much more difficult to respond compassionately to offenders. We as a church community must acknowledge our feelings. We must find ways of reaching out to the offender, offering human connectedness to aid the healing. Otherwise many of the conditions that led to the abuse—low self-esteem, poor stress management skills, learned abusive responses, and social isolation—continue. This makes future abuse likely.

In this chapter we will consider offenders. We will look at a biblical story of an offender. We will attempt to understand some of the factors which shape offenders. We will reflect on the healing and treatment necessary for abusers to end their abuse.

A Bible Story—David, the Offender

In 2 Samuel 11—12, we read of the offenses of King David. He abused members of his kingdom—Bathsheba and Uriah— people he was supposed to care for and protect. In that regard, he is similar to offenders today who harm family members.

This story occurred in the spring of the year, when David's soldiers were in battle away from Jerusalem. David himself remained at home. Late one afternoon, while walking about on the roof of his palace, he observed a beautiful woman bathing.

When he asked who the woman was, he learned she was Bathsheba, the wife of Uriah, one of his soldiers. David sent messengers to her. She came to him and he had intercourse with her.

Bathsheba returned home but soon afterward sent a message to David, "I am pregnant."

David told his battle commander, Joab, to send Uriah to him. When Uriah arrived, David inquired about the fighting, then tried to send Uriah home to his wife. Apparently David hoped Uriah would have intercourse with Bathsheba, and the pregnancy (which David was responsible for) would be attributed to Uriah.

But Uriah was loyal to his commander and fellow soldiers. "My lord Joab and the servants of my lord are camping in the open field; shall I then go to my house, to eat and to drink, and to lie with my wife? As you live, and as your soul lives, I will not do such a thing."

David tried once more, getting Uriah drunk in the hope that he would go home to Bathsheba. When that failed, David sent Uriah back to the battle with a message to Joab to arrange for Uriah to be killed in the line of duty.

Joab followed David's order. Uriah was killed. David moved swiftly to marry Bathsheba, and she bore him a son.

But David's deeds displeased the Lord. So God sent Nathan, the prophet, to David. Nathan told David a story and in doing so brought David face-to-face with his sin. Nathan pronounced the Lord's judgment on David and described the consequences David would experience because of his sin.

David acknowledged, "I have sinned." Because of his adultery and murder, David deserved the death sentence (according to the law of Moses). However, Nathan stated, "Now the Lord has put away your sin; you shall not die. Nevertheless, because by this deed you have utterly scorned the Lord, the child that is born to you shall die."

The child became sick and died. David consoled Bathsheba, went to her, and had sex with her. She bore a son, whom David named Solomon. The Lord loved the child and sent a message by Nathan, and David gave him another name, Jedidiah, "beloved of the Lord."

Reflections on the Bible Story

1. The story of David is told with the offender as the focus. It is an important story because it gives a fuller picture of King David. In this story, we see David's "shadow" side. We see his capacity for manipulation, deception, and murder.

Still, it is a partial story, for Bathsheba's perspective is not recorded. We can only imagine what Bathsheba experienced, as she was summoned by the king (is there any way she could have said no?), as she became aware of her pregnancy, as her husband was killed, as she was quickly moved from widow to wife, as she gave birth to her child and then mourned his death.

2. The text dramatically outlines the steps of David's adulterous move towards Bathsheba. "Late one afternoon . . . rose from his couch . . . walking about on the roof . . . saw . . . a woman bathing . . . the woman was . . . beautiful."

The text itself nearly seduces us into excusing David by these phrases. We can be pulled by the casual beginning of David's attraction to Bathsheba.

However, neither Bathsheba's beauty nor her public bathing was at fault. Her public bathing was not only the means of personal hygiene in those days but in this particular case was a ceremonial cleansing. "She was purifying herself after her period" (2 Samuel 11:46).

David chose to abuse his kingly power, first by summoning her to "lie with" him, then by arranging Uriah's death.

3. The religious community, in the person of Nathan, the prophet of the Lord, confronted David's sin.

4. Nathan told a story to maneuver David into owning his guilt.

5. David's sin had consequences. Life did not return to where it was. Lives were lost (Uriah's and the child's). The "sword" and "trouble" continued in David's house.

David acknowledged his sin to God. We read that he consoled Bathsheba. We do not have a record of other ways he responded to his awareness of his sin.

Making the Bible Story Our Story

1. We need to hear the stories of offenders. We need to understand the factors that have shaped them. We need to get as much information as possible regarding the offender's perspective on the abuse of power.

2. We need to hold offenders accountable for their actions. The focus must be kept on their responsibility for their behavior.

3. The religious community has a responsibility to confront offenders.

4. We need to develop wise and creative means to confront offenders. We need to find ways to break through the denial and deception practiced by perpetrators.

5. The offender must experience consequences because of the abuse. It may be the loss of relationships, as with a spouse or child.

6. Offenders need to turn from their abusiveness. Their responses must include an acknowledgement of harm done as well as repentant turning from the sin.

The Offender as Wounded Child

The abusive person carries within a wounded child. Much of the abusiveness arises from this inner child.

The inner child is the child each of us were born with and the sum of the experiences that child had in early life. We carry the child with us all the time. Sometimes we are conscious of the child. Other times the child acts on us and in us without our conscious awareness.

The child contains memories of our childhood experiences. These memories may be quite pleasant or quite traumatic depending on our experiences.

We may recognize the effect of the inner child by the presence of specific concrete memories or by less focused yet significant signals.

Let us consider a few examples.

1. I vividly recall getting wondrously wet as I worked with my sister and brothers to dam a small stream.

This is a concrete, pleasant memory.

2. While birthing my child, I experienced exquisite sensations of pleasure in between contractions. It felt as if I was floating on the most delicious bed of water. While I cannot prove it, I agree with one friend who guessed I was reliving my own experience in the womb. This is a memory more difficult to connect to a specific event.

3. Today I played a two-person competitive game with my young son. I was losing, which was okay until two other young children crowded around to watch. All of the children began to gently tease me.

I felt outnumbered. My stomach tightened. I felt threatened. I now know this emotional reaction relates to similar childhood experiences.

This is an unpleasant memory which is less focused.

4. I have an odd sensation of weakness about my upper arms and chest. When I have to move furniture, I become tense.

I now know this relates to a very painful event from my childhood. I was tricked into holding up a heavy roof for a tree house while my brother nailed it into place. My body carries with me the fear and trauma it first experienced as I held up the roof. Even though I can connect the memory to a specific event, it continues to affect me in ways that I may not realize.

I hope these illustrations help convey the power of the inner child.

Although I am now a big adult, I can quickly feel like a threatened, vulnerable child. In the same way, an abuser may be experiencing childhood memories. Only this time he becomes the great raging giant instead of the helpless victim. The emotional traumas fuel his inappropriate behaviors.

Offenders need to recognize the pain of their inner child on the path to ending their abusiveness. If we do not heal our inner child, we keep operating out of that child's pain in destructive ways. We heal the inner child, not just for our sake, but to stop the cycle of abuse. Any inner work I do is not just a gift to myself but to my children and their children and their children.

Choosing Not to Hurt Others

Yet many people have suffered horrendous childhoods and have not become abusers. In *Sexual Abuse in Christian Homes and Churches*, p. 72, Carolyn Holderread Heggen quotes psychiatrist Scott Walker, who states that victims of childhood trauma have many options for adult behavior. These may cluster around three categories: become a sheep (helpless prey to further victimization), a shepherd (a caretaker of others), or a wolf (a victimizer of others).

While we recognize that abusers may be operating from their own wounds, we do not excuse their actions. And given that many victims do not become offenders, we must look further to understand the factors influencing offenders.

Taught to Abuse

At the heart of understanding and ending family violence is a recognition that abuse is learned behavior. In family, church, and society, there are structures and power dynamics which support abuse. Abuse occurs because abusers think they have the right to abuse and know they can probably get away with it.

For the purposes of this discussion, we will consider the offender as male. (At other points in this book, I do refer to the offender as female, acknowledging such a reality.) Statistically we know that sexual abuse is primarily committed by heterosexual men against females. We also know that approximately 95 percent of the victims of domestic violence are women. (National Women Abuse Project, from Marie M. Fortune, *Violence in the Family*, p. 109.) We must attempt to understand the factors in our society that set up such abuse by men against women and children.

Below are generalizations, and there are exceptions to the rules. However, it is worthwhile to consider the truths that shape the generalizations as we work toward ending the abuse of power within the family.

1. Males tend to express themselves physically as children, then are encouraged by family and society to continue this predisposition. The interest and support given to male sports is an example of how men are encouraged to continue to express con-

flict physically and to resolve conflict by physical domination.

2. Males are also victims of physical violence. In our culture, it is expected that men will engage in physical violence as a part of being male.

3. Males are given the impossibly difficult task of suppressing their emotions (except for anger) and of always knowing how to handle every situation. Without flinching, without doubting, this ideal man is always in control, always successful. The male offender raised on this image has little hope of living up to it. Therefore, when it breaks down, he will select a target he can dominate.

4. Males are given certain privileges just because of their gender. Many men cannot recognize the ways these privileges affect their lives. Two common privileges include the opportunity of walking down the street without sexual harassment, and, on average, having a higher income than female peers.

Motivation for Abuse

There are many layers to family violence. We can benefit from further reflection about the offender's motivation for abuse.

With respect to sexual abuse, it is important to recognize the complex factors that affect one's sexuality. As we continue to work with offenders and hear their stories, we will be better able to understand their motivations.

In brief, let me offer these points.

1. Since many men do not recognize and appreciate their emotions, they have few avenues for emotional expression. Sex becomes the primary (if not sole) means of attempting to express a whole range of emotions.

This is ineffective and ultimately unsatisfying. It becomes abusive when the offender forces others into sexual activity against their will.

2. Men have few opportunities to experience touch. Because of this deficit, they may be more inclined to think of touch primarily in sexual terms and to use sex as a means of receiving other things, such as release of tension.

3. Our culture also encourages a link between sex and vio-

lence. Many movies convey this dangerous assumption. Offenders pick up this message to justify their behavior. Victims also hear the same message, then have difficulty naming the abuse because it fits the cultural norm.

Let us broaden our discussion to include offenders who abuse physically and emotionally as well as sexually.

It is important to recognize that much of what motivates an offender's behavior is his need to control. The "Power and Control Wheel" (at the end of the chapter) demonstrates the different abuses the offender inflicts, all with the purpose of dominating the victim.

Offenders tend to have rigid, "traditional" views about the family, about religion, about the roles of men and women and parents and children. These rigid views feed into and continue the abuse, as the abuser attempts to maintain control over his spouse and children. He does not accept challenges to his "authority" or demonstrate ability to relate to family members as individuals.

Final Comments Regarding Abusers' Characteristics

1. Offenders tend to have low-self esteem. Sexual abusers are extremely insecure. They also typically have poor sexual self-esteem. This means they do not feel healthy and balanced with respect to their sexuality. Their sexual understandings are immature, based on their own damaged sexual experiences, pornography, and the media. They have tended not to have satisfying intimate relationships.

Physically abusive men do not feel good about themselves. Insecurity makes them sensitive to and rejected by criticism. Again, the physical violence is a means of keeping anxiety-producing stimuli under control, which means the behaviors of spouse and children are controlled by him.

2. Abusers do not have a good network of friends. In many cases, they are dependent on their wives for forming and maintaining their social networks. Alternatively, they may know a great many people, because of their public presence, yet they may not really be known by anyone. They have difficulty being intimate. Their isolation increases the likelihood that they will abuse.

3. Some offenders are also drug or alcohol abusers. The substance abuse does not cause the physical violence. The offender cannot blame his violence on the substance abuse. However, in his altered state he may inflict injuries in a more frequent or severe manner. He may use his substance abuse to avoid taking responsibility for his actions.

4. Offenders share a tendency to deny. They lie about their abuse or minimize the consequences of their actions. This denial can be genuine in that some abusers practice deception so regularly that they convince even themselves. Or they may have acted in such an alcoholic fog that they do not remember.

If their denial is conscious, it can be motivated by wanting to save face or avoid legal consequences. Then again, facing the consequences of their actions is a formidable prospect. Sex offenders, particularly those who have molested children, are at risk of being sexually assaulted in prison.

All of these "reasons" for abuse are not acceptable. Each offender must take responsibility for the abuse and turn from continuing the abusive pattern. Abusers must learn new, healthy ways of living.

Healing, Treatment, Recovery

What does the healing journey look like for an offender? What treatment is necessary? How does the offender stop abusing others? What does it mean in spiritual terms? There are a number of steps the offender needs to take.

Accepting Responsibility for the Offense

Currently, most offenders must be convicted of an offense before they will seek help. A few offenders do voluntarily turn themselves into the authorities and/or seek treatment. While these people are in the minority, their initiative is commendable. They are also more likely to benefit from treatment because they are acknowledging they have a problem.

Even so, offenders who are court-ordered into treatment, particularly into groups of offenders, benefit from such treatment. It is difficult to accept responsibility for such damaging actions, yet it is the cornerstone for change.

Empathizing with the Victim

At some point in the healing, the recovering offender needs to open himself to the full impact of his actions on the survivor. This may happen by the offender telling the story of the abuse from first his perspective, then from the survivor's perspective.

In some programs, survivors meet directly with offenders. These rare exchanges are healing for survivors if they have initiated or chosen such contact. The experience tends to be informative and helpful for both groups, even if it is not a meeting of offenders with their victims.

Many offenders find healing by making statements of remorse to their victims. Restitution, a financial response to victims, is another way to express remorse. Restitution symbolizes abusers' desire to respond to the harm they have caused. It is symbolic because what is lost cannot be restored in many cases. Even so, it is a significant symbol.

Building a Network

Offenders often must learn friendship skills. Because of their isolation, they need to develop tools to build friends. For many offenders, this means learning to initiate social events, taking risks in sharing feelings, relaxing and having fun with others.

If the legal system has been involved, there may have been a conviction with a jail sentence. There may also be a loss of work, income, home, and family. The offender often faces overwhelming obstacles after disclosure.

Appropriate Tools for Managing Stress and Anger

Some of the offender's wrong behaviors may stem from an inability to cope with daily stress appropriately. Offenders respond to the stress by hurting others. Offenders need to identify the emotions of stress and anger in early stages, explore the range of optional behaviors available to them, and implement alternatives to their previously abusive behaviors.

The Use of Power

People who have abused their power in intimate relationships must learn to back off. Previously they used their power forcefully and violently. Now they must learn to hold their power in check. They must not force contact with their victims or demand particular responses from their victims. Because of the violation of power, requests from the offender are heard by the victim as an obligation or another demand. Even a request for forgiveness can appear to some survivors as a further demand.

See the Equality Wheel (figure 6-2) for how an offender works toward nonviolence in relationships.

Spiritual Journey

The psalmist expresses the misery noted by some offenders. (Note that some versions indicate David wrote this psalm after his abuse of Bathsheba and Uriah.)

> While I kept silence, my body wasted away
> through my groaning all day long.
>   For day and night your hand was heavy
> upon me; my strength was dried up as by the
> heat of summer.
>   Then I acknowledged my sin to you,
> and I did not hide my iniquity;
>   I said, "I will confess my transgressions
> to the Lord," and you forgave the guilt of my sin.
>   (Ps. 32:3-5)

The offender must make his spiritual peace. The church can both aid and hinder this process. Because of our Christian understandings of God's forgiveness, the offender is offered a means of moving on from his sins. All of us have been graced with the assurance of God's pardon, after we confess and repent of our sins. Offenders can likewise avail themselves of such grace.

However, the process of forgiveness and reconciliation with others is not well-defined or simple. Survivors and others require time. Forgiveness and reconciliation are not automatic or speedy. Neither offenders nor survivors are helped by being forced into a premature reconciliation (see chapter 12 for further comment).

Many churches are not able to provide offenders with a

strong support network that can both call offenders to accountability and surround them with Christian compassion. Churches cannot simply avoid their responsibility to the offenders in their midst. They must develop a means of responding. Even so, offenders must often spend time in the desert wrestling with their souls. There they may find God.

Summary

In spite of our stereotypes, offenders are not generally rough-looking strangers who linger around parks and dark alleys waiting to pounce on the vulnerable. They are our neighbors, our church leaders, our aunts, our grandfathers, and our Sunday school teachers. They look like normal people.

Offenders are human beings, capable of good, who choose for a variety of reasons to participate in evil. The church community must call offenders to repent and turn from their lives of sin.

Prayer

Dear God,

We acknowledge a range of human reactions in response to offenders. We may see ourselves in them and do not like what we see. We may hate them and wish to ban them from our lives, our families, our churches. We may so closely identify with them that we are unable clearly to name their abuse as sin.

Open our eyes that we may firmly denounce the sin of family violence. Open our hearts that we may love the offender as you do. Amen.

Discussion Questions

1. Imagine that you have just discovered your church elder, a person you respect, is a family violence offender. What is your initial response? What do you feel and do? How would your church likely respond if the information was public?

2. What resources would you like to see your church put in place for responding to offenders?

3. What relationships have you had with offenders? What are your emotions in such relationships?

4. What use of your own power in family relationships makes

you uncomfortable? What supports do you need to choose healthy Christlike actions more readily?

Resources

Alsdurf, James and Phyllis Alsdurf, "What Kind of Men Abuse Their Wives," *Battered into Submission: The Tragedy of Wife Abuse in the Christian Home*.

Carnes, Patrick, *Out of the Shadows*.

Heggen, Carolyn Holderread, "The Perpetrator," *Sexual Abuse in Christian Families and Churches*.

Rutter, Peter, *Sex in the Forbidden Zone*.

Sonkin, Daniel J. and Michael Durphy, *Learning to Live Without Violence*.

Figure 6-1.

Used by permission of
Domestic Abuse Intervention Project

206 West Fourth Street
Duluth, Minnesota 55806

218 722-4134

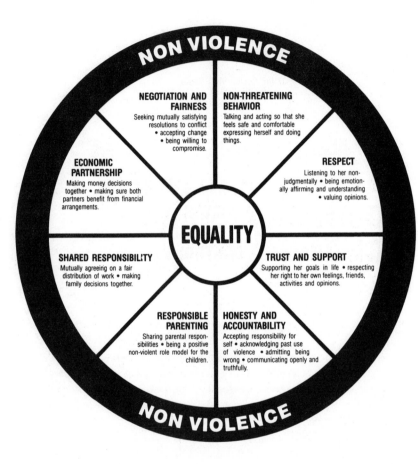

Figure 6-2.

Used by permission of
Domestic Abuse Intervention Project

206 West Fourth Street
Duluth, Minnesota 55806

218 722-4134

7

A Challenge to the Compassionate Church

LARNEL CLOSED his eyes and faithfully followed his counselor's instructions. Six months previously Larnel had remembered the brutal sexual assault he had experienced as a six-year-old. Together he and James, the counselor, had worked through the memories. James now wanted to bring closure to the trauma, and James suggested religious imagery. Larnel, a deeply committed Christian, agreed.

As he sat with eyes closed, he relaxed readily. James had a deep, warm, calming voice. James also had dark chocolate skin and a large rounded body. In some ways he reminded Larnel of his grandmother, whom he loved deeply. Larnel trusted James.

James instructed him to remember the basement where the rape occurred. Larnel imagined the dark room with the hard floor. He felt the pain and kept breathing, holding on to the steadiness of James' voice.

"Look at your six-year-old boy in the basement."

Larnel saw his younger self, sobbing and devastated.

"Now picture Jesus in the basement with your little boy."

Larnel searched the dark room for the comforting presence of Christ. He could not find him. His little boy remained alone and abandoned.

Larnel signaled this information to James.

James switched directions, "In your adult form, make contact with your little Larnel. In some way, let him know that you care about him."

Larnel imagined stretching out a hand to his hurt boy and squeezing him on the shoulder. "I'll be back," he promised.

James drew Larnel into the present by instructing him to gradually become aware of his breathing, then open his eyes.

James looked intently at Larnel and asked, "What was that like for you?"

"God wasn't there," Larnel replied wistfully. "No one was there."

* * * * * * * * * *

Introduction

The trauma experienced by many survivors is felt in their faith walk. Witnesses often are ill prepared to accompany survivors in their faith struggles. Consider Larnel's experience of the absence of God. The person who has had such an experience is deeply troubled. With other great traumas, one's first inclination is to avoid, run away from, or deny. It hurts too much to stay in contact with a place where God is absent.

Those of us without such an experience are inclined to deny it. "God is everywhere," we declare. We too are motivated by a fear of the prospect of living in a world without God.

Healing for the survivor of family violence requires honesty. The survivor must be faithful to the memory of the event. In Larnel's case, that meant faithfully recalling the utter aloneness of his six-year-old. It is difficult for survivors to hold fast to such a terrible memory, and difficult for witnesses to listen to such an account. Yet to fully respond to family violence, we must listen to the agony.

In this chapter we take another step into understanding some of the difficult faith questions related to family violence.

A Bible Story—The Rape and Death of the Levite's Concubine

In Judges 19–21 we read the story of the rape and death of an unnamed woman, known only as the Levite's concubine.

The concubine lived with her husband, a Levite, in a remote area in the hill country of Ephraim. She became angry with him and went to her father's house at Bethlehem in Judah. After four months the Levite went to her to speak tenderly to her and bring her back. He traveled with his servant and a couple of donkeys.

When he reached her father's house, he was warmly welcomed by his father-in-law. The two men spent several days and nights eating and drinking.

The Levite finally extricated himself late on the afternoon of the fifth day. He had spent the earlier part of the day eating and drinking with his father-in-law. In spite of his father-in-law's protests, he was unwilling to stay another night and departed with his donkeys, his concubine, and his servant.

It was dangerous to sleep out in the unprotected countryside. The servant urged the Levite to stop at Jebus, a "city of foreigners." But the Levite insisted that they hurry on to Gibeah, an Israelite city, where Benjaminites lived. They reached the city square at sunset.

They were counting on Middle East hospitality, assured that someone would offer them shelter for the night. But for some time they were left alone in the city square. Finally an old man, originally from the same hill country as the Levite and now living in Gibeah, offered hospitality. The old man took in the Levite, his concubine, his servant, and his donkeys. They refreshed themselves and sat down to enjoy food and drink.

Then some of the wicked men of the city surrounded the house. Pounding on the door, they shouted to the old man, "Bring out the man who came into your house, so that we may have intercourse with him."

The owner of the house went outside and tried to dissuade them, "No, my brothers, do not act so wickedly. Since this man is my guest, do not do this vile thing. Here are my virgin daughter and his concubine; let me bring them out now. Ravish them and do whatever you want to them; but against this man do not do such a vile thing."

But the men would not listen to him. So the Levite seized his concubine and put her out to them. They wantonly raped her and abused her throughout the night. At dawn they let her go.

As morning approached, the woman went back to the house where her master was staying, fell down at the door, and lay there until it was light.

Her master got up in the morning and opened the door. There was his concubine lying at the door of the house, with her hands on the threshold. "Get up," he said to her, "we are going." But there was no answer. Then he put her on his donkey and set out for his home.

When he reached home, he took a knife and cut up his concubine, limb by limb, into twelve parts. He sent her body parts into all the areas of Israel. He commanded the men whom he sent, "Thus shall you say to all the Israelites, 'Has such a thing ever happened since the day that the Israelites came up from the land of Egypt until this day? Consider it, take counsel, and speak out.' "

The Israelites (except for the Benjaminites) gathered to consider their response. They heard the Levite's account of the events. They then vowed war on the Benjaminites. They first asked the Benjaminites to "hand over those scoundrels in Gibeah, so that we may put them to death, and purge the evil from Israel."

The Benjaminites would not listen to their fellow Israelites, so they united to fight. After three days of fighting, the Benjaminites were defeated. Six hundred Benjaminites men fled into the desert, but the Israelites destroyed the Benjaminites towns, including the people and the animals.

Then the Israelites grieved for their brothers, the Benjaminites. "One tribe is cut off from Israel. . . What shall we do for wives for those who are left?" The book of Judges ends with the Israelites—through more bloodshed, trickery, and kidnapping—procuring wives for their Benjamite relatives so they can rebuild their tribe.

Reflections on the Story

1. This final story in the book of Judges summarizes much of the history of that period. The last verse of Judges reads, "In those days there was no king in Israel; all the people did what was right in their own eyes" (21:25). It was a chaotic, violent time.

2. The text is disturbingly unclear as to what was "the awful thing." To our eyes, the gang rape of the concubine and her dismemberment by her husband are most gruesome.

The text seems to suggest that it is the threat of violence (sexual and physical) toward the Levite which was disgraceful. The old man who hosted the Levite offered both his own young daughter and the Levite's concubine to the marauders who wanted to assault sexually the Levite. When the wicked men continued to threaten, the Levite put his concubine out to them. The men's lives and bodies were considered of higher value than the women's.

3. The concubine was shown no mercy, neither by the men who abused her nor by her husband. Her last conscious act appears to have been to stretch out her hands on the threshold.

4. Concubines, like other women and slaves, were considered property. The Levite's anger does not seem to be motivated by compassion toward his concubine. Another interpretation is that his anger arose because of the damage to his property (the concubine). Is that the source of the rage that resulted in his sending her body pieces to the twelve tribes?

5. It appears difficult to find the presence of God in such horror.

Making the Bible Story Our Story

1. Many survivors of family violence find themselves questioning the presence of God. Consider this survivor's psalm.

> My thoughts are quiet.
> I call on my Lord and God.
> Does she hear me?
> Do I feel her presence?

What is that feeling—
peace, calm?

Where is the peace and calm
when my thoughts are full of turmoil,
when my stomach churns,
when my heart races in fear,
when panic rises in my chest,
when anger is burning in my stomach?

My God, where are you then?

Most survivors have experienced some of the powerlessness that the Levite's concubine experienced. Children, women, persons of color, disabled people, and many more find themselves vulnerable to being threatened and abused.

Like the concubine, someone else's life is valued above theirs. A white person. A male. A person with strong legs who can run away. These people, like the Levite and his elderly host, can protect themselves by sending out a less powerful one to the wicked men, then shutting the door to sleep securely.

In her final night, the concubine experienced hell. This is the experience of other survivors of family violence. The horror and violation they encounter in their own bodies and souls is hell. In the moments of the abuse, there is no compassion, no refuge, no mercy.

2. The Levite and his servant expected the normal rules of hospitality to apply. As strangers in the city, it was reasonable to expect that they would be taken in and welcomed and protected according to the Hebrew hospitality code. An Arabic Bedouin proverb states, "The one who shares my bread and my salt is not my enemy." They trusted the normal structures of society.

We also trust the normal structures. Parents nurture their children. Older relatives respect the sexual boundaries of younger family members. Husbands love their wives "as their own bodies." But in family violence the chaos of evil overtakes the normal structures.

Listening to the Vulnerable Ones

The story of the brutality experienced by the Levite's concubine is one of the most horrible accounts imaginable. It is difficult to hear it and reflect on its meaning.

I include it in this chapter to set the context for the challenge of the compassionate church. To heal the family violence in our midst, the church must listen and be instructed by survivors and repentant offenders. Their direct experience with family violence guides us in our justice-making and healing, and their faith perspectives can enrich the entire church.

The Christian church has a noble tradition of responding to the weak and the vulnerable. It has advocated for the disadvantaged, the poor, and the sick. However, this tradition has not extended to the victims of family violence. Today the church is being challenged to embrace family violence survivors with the Christlike compassion shown to other vulnerable people.

Compassion is a strong, active love. At its root, compassion means "to suffer with." To act compassionately, Christians must suffer with the victims of violence. One form of compassion is to listen to their horror stories and faith questions, even when this is excruciatingly difficult.

At this point in our corporate response to family violence, we are blessed to have the strong and articulate voices of a number of survivors. They challenge the church to consider Christian teachings and church life from their perspectives.

The faith journey of each person is shaped by life experiences; at the same time our faith shapes our lives. In our churches, we have heard more from the "dominant view" of the powerful ones. Our sermons, our seminaries, our church leaders, and our biblical interpretation for hundreds of years have been shaded by the perspective of the dominant.

Think for the moment on how these two perspectives (the dominant and the vulnerable) view the story differently. Imagine the story first from the concubine's eyes. Then imagine the story from the Levite's perspective. The one story seems split into two entirely different stories. But this story is primarily told in the Bible from the Levite's perspective.

Even in the text we see some of this shift. When the Levite

tells the story to the assembled Israelites, he alters the text in slight but significant ways. He says the Gibeans intended to kill him (rather than sexually assault him). Then he omits the fact that he sent the concubine out to the men (his contribution to her assault). He simply states that they raped her, and she died.

Many survivors of family violence live with these shifts in perspective as a regular reality in their faith walk. Often the public level of church discussion does not address their experiences.

A Few Examples

1. Some survivors are understandably troubled by the hypocrisy of their offenders and of their churches. Often survivors attend the same church as their offenders. How does a survivor feel when the offender preaches, offers prayer, or serves communion? How is a survivor protected when an offender continues to lead the church in visible, public ways? How does a survivor make sense of her faith journey when her offender continues to appear publicly as a "man of God"?

2. Reflect on these verses from James 1:2-3. "My brothers and sisters, whenever you face trials of any kind, consider it nothing but joy, because you know that the testing of your faith produces endurance."

A pastor preaching on this text may exhort listeners to cheerfully press on in the normal ups and downs of being a Christian. How does this approach sound to a man who has been emotionally abused by his wife the previous evening? He may well hear it as a directive to return for more abuse.

3. Reflect on the concept of submission. Generally submission means "dying to self" and obeying God's will. This term sounds different to a person living in an abusive situation than it does to a person with no experience of such abusiveness.

4. In some churches, an emphasis is placed on the cross and suffering. Believers are exhorted, "Pick up your cross" and "Suffer as Jesus did." How does this sound to an elderly man who is being deprived of his income?

5. Many survivors experience times when the emotions associated with the violence are quite intense and demanding. There is rarely a place in the church where survivors can express these emotions.

Instead church life is often structured to tell us what to believe, how to pray, and the points of correct doctrine. This intellectual approach is often at odds with the emotional experiences of survivors.

6. For some survivors, it is not comforting to turn to images of God as father. In fact, the domination of the church by men and by language and faith teachings based primarily on male experience can become an obstacle to their healing. The church does not offer solace because it is too defining, too restrictive, too reminiscent of the circumstances surrounding their abuse.

By listening to survivors, we learn what church and Christianity is like for them. This can challenge our most cherished beliefs. Our tendency may be to hold even tighter to our dogmas and beliefs. However, we need to enter into the swirling chaos and find God in the upheaval.

Learning from Offenders

The compassionate church also needs to listen to offenders. Repentant offenders can enrich our faith journey and guide our responses to family violence. A man who has violated a family member, been confronted with his offense, acknowledged his full responsibility, and changed his ways can share from his experience in a helpful way.

How did he experience God along the way? What did he learn about listening to the vulnerable ones? How does the church misguide him in his use of power? How can the church support him in using his power appropriately? What can he tell us about forgiveness and reconciliation?

We must not block out the voices of repentant offenders.

Prayer

Dear God,

How do we pray when the evil snuffs out all signs of you? Our spirits wail and groan with the horror we witness. We seek your presence. Amen.

Discussion Questions

1. Take time to debrief your reaction to the Bible story. In a safe setting, discuss your feelings.

2. Discuss times when it has been difficult for you to find the presence of God. What resources helped you live through or come out of such times?

3. How do you find yourself aligned with the dominant perspective? How do you find yourself aligned with the minority, or vulnerable, perspective?

4. What hinders you from listening and being compassionate to the vulnerable ones? What helps you to listen and be compassionate?

5. Reflect on ways survivors may experience discomfort in church. What is your reaction to such examples? How do you find it difficult to change for the sake of survivors? What ingredients of your worship style or language can you modify to accommodate survivors?

Resources

Trible, Phyllis, "An Unnamed Woman: The Extravagance of Violence," *Texts of Terror*.

8

Resolutions

Vincent is an elder at a large Protestant church. As part of his responsibilities, he serves on the youth ministry team. In the last six months he and his co-workers have been dealing with a number of troubled teens. Paul, long quiet and withdrawn, confided to Vincent that his father is physically abusive; Paul fears for his and his mother's safety. Mercedes told the youth pastor that she was sexually assaulted by a cousin the previous summer. Now Charles, who has been disruptive and aggressive, is charged with two counts of sexual assault for "pinching girls' buns at school."

Vincent feels shocked, angry, and frightened. At the same time he wants to provide strong, compassionate leadership to these young people. "Where do I turn?" he wonders.

Introduction

Across North America, church leaders like Vincent are finding themselves inundated with innumerable situations of family violence and sexual abuse. When they hear of current abuses in their congregations, they react in much the same way as other people—with shock, denial, horror, anger. Yet because of their position or spiritual maturity, they find themselves having to hold out hope and encouragement to others. What do we do when confronted with overwhelming evil?

In this chapter we ask several Bible passages to guide us.

Psalms

The Psalms are a particular source of comfort. The Psalms are a musical or poetic account of God's relationship with the Israelites. Written over a number of centuries, they were likely compiled in their current form from the fourth to the second centuries B.C. They are a Jewish hymnbook. Like good music anywhere, they express human experiences and emotions. The writers of the Psalms do not shirk from communicating great sorrow as well as great joy. These poets were able to convey the sadness that accompanies personal attacks and personal losses.

Consider these passages.

> All who hate me whisper together about me;
>> they imagine the worst for me.
> They think that a deadly thing has fastened on me,
>> that I will not rise again from where I lie.
> Even my bosom friend in whom I trusted,
>> who ate of my bread, has lifted the heel against me.
>> (Psalm 41:7-9)

> [O Lord], you have put me in the depths of the Pit,
>> in the regions dark and deep.
> Your wrath lies heavy upon me,
>> and you overwhelm me with all your waves.
> O Lord, why do you cast me off?
>> Why do you hide your face from me?
> Wretched and close to death from my youth up,
>> I suffer your terrors; I am desperate.
> Your wrath has swept over me;
>> your dread assaults destroy me.
> They surround me like a flood all day long;
>> from all sides they close in on me.
> You have caused friend and neighbor to shun me;
>> my companions are in darkness.
>> (Psalm 88:6-7, 14-18)

The Psalms offer us a vehicle to express our deepest feelings. Lamenting is a means of grieving, of expressing our sorrow, of mourning.

Lamenting is not encouraged in the Christian church. We are urged to move through grief as swiftly as possible. One yearly experience of lamenting occurs when we somberly acknowledge Good Friday (and in some denominations, the entire forty days of Lent). But Easter follows swiftly and we move briskly into the spring sunshine and the joy of the resurrection. This is good. Our Christian faith is built on this foundation of the resurrected Christ.

However, in the journey of ministering to those damaged by family violence, we must allow for lamenting. For many individuals, victims and offenders, that means months and years of grieving. Railing against God. Intense fury seeking a secure channel. Sadness for the losses. The Psalms give us a language in which to lament.

The Psalms also regularly point us back to God. According to the psalmist, God cares about the poor and the lowly and rewards those who aid the dispossessed. God the source of our being is our savior, our refuge, and our strength.

Along with the psalmist, we commit ourselves to caring for the poor and the powerless (the victims of family violence). We also keep sight of the larger picture, trusting in a God of justice who restores balance to this unbalanced world.

Matthew

At that time the disciples came to Jesus and asked, "Who is the greatest in the kingdom of heaven?"

He called a child, whom he put among them, and said, "Truly I tell you, unless you change and become like children, you will never enter the kingdom of heaven. Whoever becomes humble like this child is the greatest in the kingdom of heaven. Whoever welcomes one such child in my name welcomes me.

"If any of you put a stumbling block before one of these little ones who believe in me, it would be better for you if a great millstone were fastened around your neck and you were drowned in the depth of the sea. Woe to the world because of stumbling blocks! Occasions for stumbling are bound to come, but woe to the one by whom the stumbling block comes!

"If your hand or your foot causes you to stumble, cut it off and throw it away; it is better for you to enter life maimed or lame than to have two hands or two feet and to be thrown into the eternal fire. And if your eye causes you to stumble, tear it out and throw it away; it is better for you to enter life with one eye than to have two eyes and to be thrown into the hell of fire. (Matt. 18:1-9)

In this passage Jesus makes strong statements about children, power, and offenders.

The story begins with Jesus' disciples engaged in their ongoing quest to determine greatest. They wanted to figure who was number one (or who would be) and in what relation they would be to whoever emerged as number one.

Jesus had been working hard with the disciples, trying to make a point about power. In Matthew 16:13-28, Jesus quizzed the disciples about his identity. Peter correctly confessed, "You are the Messiah, the Son of the living God."

From that point on, Jesus taught his disciples that he must go to Jerusalem, suffer, and die. He challenged his disciples, "If any want to become my followers, let them deny themselves, and take up their cross and follow me."

The Jesus way was not about earthly kingdoms, hierarchies, and grabbing power. Although Jesus proclaimed his message faithfully, the disciples, like us, were slow to catch on. The disciples were anxious to determine "the greatest in the kingdom" and who would "sit on [Jesus'] right hand." We might see in their questions a parallel with current attempts to set up "chains of command" or calls for obedience to "male authority."

This time when the disciples asked the anxious question, Jesus tried an object lesson. As in this case, Jesus often gave indirect answers. When asked a question, he replied with a story or riddle, leaving the questioner to stew in the original question plus Jesus' oblique answer.

Placing a child in their midst, Jesus said, "Truly I tell you, unless you change and become like children, you will never enter the kingdom of heaven." (Forget about being the greatest!)

He continued, "Whoever becomes humble like this child, is the greatest in the kingdom of heaven."

Jesus tried to broaden the disciples' constricted views of

power and greatness. He held out a vision of living in which humility was greatness and the powerless become the leaders. His answer also suggests that no one person is the *greatest*, but that *greatness* is characteristic of the humble.

In the same passage, Jesus affirmed those who welcomed children in his name. And he issued a severe warning to anyone who "puts a stumbling block before one of these little ones." Jesus declared, "It would be better for you if a great millstone were fastened around your neck and you were drowned in the depth of the sea." We cannot read these forceful words of Jesus without applying them to the children harmed by family violence. Jesus steadfastly condemned the abuse of children.

Jesus instructed, "If your hand or foot causes you to stumble, cut it off and throw it away." It is difficult to determine the precise intent of these hard words. It is hard to imagine Jesus commanding people to mutilate their bodies.

It does seem reasonable to conclude that Jesus was sending an unambiguous message to offenders. "You are responsible for the actions of your body. Don't blame your victims. You are the one who should suffer consequences—and cease offending."

Ephesians

Be subject to one another out of reverence for Christ.

Wives, be subject to your husbands as you are to the Lord. For the husband is the head of the wife just as Christ is the head of the church, the body of which he is the Savior. Just as the church is subject to Christ, so also wives are to be, in everything, to their husbands.

Husbands, love your wives just as Christ loved the church and gave himself up for her, in order to make her holy by cleansing her with the washing of the water by the word, so as to present the church to himself in splendor, without a spot or wrinkle or anything of the kind—yes, so that she may be holy and without blemish.

In the same way, husbands should love their wives as they do their own bodies. He who loves his wife loves himself. For no one ever hates his own body, but he nourishes and tenderly cares for it, just as Christ does for the church, because we are members of his body.

"For this reason a man will leave his father and mother and be joined to his wife, and the two will become one flesh." This is a great mystery, and I am applying it to Christ and the church. Each of you, however, should love his wife as himself, and a wife should respect her husband.

Children, obey your parents in the Lord, for this is right. "Honor your father and mother"—this is the first commandment with a promise: "so that it may be well with you and you may live long on the earth."

And fathers, do not provoke your children to anger, but bring them up in the discipline and instruction of the Lord. (Eph. 5:21–6:4)

This passage is popularly seen as Christian instruction for family life. Many speakers focus on the wife's duty to submit to her husband. This focus is somewhat curious considering that the opening statement, which seems to summarize the main intent of the whole passage, is clearly directed to everybody—husbands, wives, children, parents. "Be subject to one another out of reverence for Christ" (5:21)

Emphasizing wifely submission is also a slanted reading. Consider the number of verses geared specifically to husbands (nine) as compared to the number of verses geared specifically to wives (three).

This passage of Scripture clearly instructs families to practice the mutual submission Jesus modeled. Submission means "give way to" or "accommodate." As mentioned earlier, Jesus envisioned a kingdom where the power imbalances would be righted. He himself, as teacher and rabbi, showed by washing the disciples' feet that leaders serve. In his reign, "the first shall be last and the last shall be first."

These verses from Ephesians follow in that tradition. This early Christian writer encouraged the fledgling church members to model their family relationships on mutual submission.

No one individual is greater than another. No single spouse, parent, or child lords it over the other. By directing wives to submit, husbands to love, children to honor, and parents (fathers) to avoid provoking their children to anger, the writer was telling these families, "Each person is equally important. Each must use their power respectfully. Each must accommodate the other."

Consider the verses carefully. The writer seems to recognize the worth of each person. Remember that in this culture women and children are considered the *property* of men.

Yet the writer speaks to them, directs remarks to them, not as if they were pieces of property, but as if they were human beings with free will and conscious choice. The writer urges these (formerly dispossessed) people to choose submission.

Furthermore, the writer challenges the husbands and fathers who had virtually unquestioned power in those days. The writer upends the power structure by instructing the powerful ones in the same way—choose submission.

If we carefully read the instructions to husbands, we clearly see the call to share power respectfully. "Love your wives just as Christ loved the church and gave himself up for her" and "Love [your] wives as . . . [your] own bodies." These examples all push out the meaning of the mutual submission first described in verse 21.

Husbands are instructed to love their wives as Christ loved the church and gave himself up for her. How did Christ give himself up for her? By dying for her—the ultimate act of submission.

I am not recommending that husbands literally die for their wives. Although I do chuckle when some spouses declare, "Of course I'll *die* for you. Just don't ask me to make supper for you or look after the kids." We often prefer the unachievable noble act to the daily small act of service.

It appears that the writer is giving husbands an example of ultimate submission to impress on them the full significance of the directive. Be prepared to die to self, to accommodate your wife, to set aside your agenda as a way of demonstrating your Christlike love. These verses truly herald a revolutionary change in family relationships.

We see the theme of mutual respect in a Bible passage that specifically addressed marital sexual relations. In 1 Corinthians 7:3-4 we read,

> The husband should give to his wife her conjugal rights, and likewise the wife to her husband. For the wife does not have authority over her own body, but the husband does; likewise the husband does not have authority over his own body, but the wife does.

These Bible verses point toward sexual relationships that are mutual, respectful, and consenting. Marital rape and coerced sexual activity has no place in the Christian marriage.

The few verses that speak specifically to parent-child relationships continue the theme. The children are to honor their parents, a restatement of the Hebrew commandment "that your days may be long upon the earth." Note that the child is instructed to honor "in the Lord." Blind obedience is not being commanded.

Yet the instructions to the parents (fathers) offer a corrective to the possible misuse of the commandment. For the fathers are instructed not to provoke their children to anger. Again this signals a major shift in thinking about the father's role. He is to take care with his power that the children are not violated, not pushed to exasperation or anger. He is given a positive instruction to "bring them up in the discipline and instruction of the Lord" (see chapter 2 for a discussion of Christian discipline.)

Husbands and fathers—those who previously ruled with unlimited power—are guided into new relationships of shared power.

We again turn to Jesus for a glimpse of how Jesus envisioned his relationship with his heavenly parent. In Matthew 7:9-11, Jesus drew a parallel between human family relationships and God's care for us.

> "Is there anyone among you who,
> if your child asks for bread, will give a stone?
>   Or if the child asks for a fish,
> will give a snake?
>   If you then who are evil,
> know how to give good gifts to your children,
> how much more will your Father in heaven
> give good things to those who ask him!"

Jesus seems to expect family relationships to be based on the parents sensitively responding to the child's needs.

Make the Bible Story Our Story

How do we apply these Bible references to our specific experiences with family violence? Let us consider a few stories.

1. Eli regretted his first fifteen years of parenting. With a half dozen hungry, growing children, Eli scrambled to keep steady employment as a construction laborer and serve his church as a lay pastor. He felt stretched thin all the time, at work, at church, and at home. All too often, his children suffered from his frequent absences and his infrequent but violent outbursts.

As his oldest children became teenagers, Eli sadly realized he did not have the relationship he needed to nurture his children into adulthood. Their rebelliousness seemed directly linked to the anger provoked by his earlier violence.

Eli repented. He reoriented his life, reduced his church work, and enjoyed more leisurely, pleasant interactions with his younger children. He apologized to his older children, and, as they became adults, they accepted his invitations to visit and talk. By word and example he signaled his intention to be a compassionate, responsive parent.

Eli took his new cues from the biblical instructions to avoid provoking his children's anger, and to bring them up in the discipline and instruction of the Lord.

2. Anneliese no longer trusted herself around her elderly mother. She had known she was tense but did not realize how close she was to violence until the previous week.

Anneliese had finally settled her mother into the living room after what seemed like hours of fussing over her. Helping her bathe and dress. Fixing her hair. Making her lunch which was never good enough. Arranging her chair and her footstool. Anneliese set a glass of grape juice on the end table near her mother, turned on a television program her mother liked, then left the room to eat her own lunch.

Fifteen minutes later she checked around the corner. She exploded as she saw the spilled grape juice dripping onto the peach and gray sofa. "Mother!" she screamed. "What's wrong with you?" She drew back her hand, wanting to slap her mother with the force of her rage. Somehow she stopped herself and directed her energy into cleaning the stain.

Anneliese was frightened by her anger. She recognized that she now had power over her mother and was becoming abusive with her power. She turned to her eldest son for help. They had always been close and she trusted his advice. He quickly encouraged her to contact their pastor, who directed her to an organization that assisted caregivers of the elderly.

There Anneliese learned to recognize her stresses. She worried about her daughter's divorce, and her grandson quitting school, in addition to carrying the full responsibility for her mother's care. She also recalled her mother's emotional abuse from earlier years, and realized that some of her mother's current comments were triggers for those past hurts.

Anneliese developed ways to manage her stress. Most important was setting up alternate caregivers. Anneliese's brothers each came one afternoon a week and each of her children agreed to also look after Grandma for a weekly four-hour shift.

Anneliese turned to the Psalms to express her pain from her wounded childhood. After several months of meditating, she felt an urge to paint. She enrolled in a watercolors class and found healing through a series of paintings she created.

When her mother died three years later, Anneliese was able to bury her peacefully, without guilt and regrets. She had been able to respond to her mother with the mutual submission described in Ephesians.

3. Valentina always associated her incest experience with oppressive church structures. She believed that the church of her youth hated women, or at least was extremely uncomfortable with them.

"What else could it mean when the pastor said, 'Women cannot preach because sin entered the world first through a woman'?" she questioned. "Or why were wives told to submit to their husbands, when husbands were not instructed to be equally accommodating?"

Valentina believed she was molested by her older male cousins "because I was female—and unprotected. The whole message of the culture was that women were to serve men, that was their entire reason to exist."

When she became an adult, she looked for a church where, in

her words, "men and women are equal, where power and authority is not considered an assumed privilege based solely on gender, where God is believed to be loving and not judgmental, and where it is recognized that all people are made equal in God's image."

When Valentina found such a church, she experienced God's love through her relationships with Christians who modeled mutual submission and shared power. This matched her understanding of Jesus' teachings.

Summary

We can find biblical guidance in the midst of confronting family violence. From the three passages we considered in detail, we can hold on to these principles.

1. Humility, mutual submission, and shared power express the Jesus way for Christian families.

2. We offer a vision of right, just relationships. We believe that this is what God intends for the whole world, including Christian families.

3. The abuse of children is condemned explicitly. We can safely assume that abuse has no place in any family relationship.

4. Offenders bear the responsibility for their actions.

5. Laments are particularly needed. We must find vehicles to express our deep mourning.

6. God accepts our anguish.

7. The thrust of the Bible is a challenge to a status quo built on hierarchies, oppressive domination, and crushing powerlessness. True followers of Christ accept his revolutionary call.

Prayer

Dear God,

The waves of family violence threaten to engulf us, smothering all sense of your presence. We thank you for your written word, which has guided your faithful followers over the centuries. We ask you to open our hearts to the meaning of the Scriptures as we respond to family violence today. Amen.

Discussion Questions

1. When have you needed to lament or mourn? How did your church community assist you or hinder you in your attempts to lament? What Bible resources did you find helpful?

2. How do you express anguish to God?

3. Consider the interpretation of the Matthew 18 passage about the children coming to Jesus. In your life and in your daily family relationships, how do you apply Jesus's teaching that we must become humble like children rather than competing to be the greatest?

4. Has your understanding of marriage relationships or parenting relationships changed? If so, in what ways?

5. What do you think God expects of us in our family relationships? Consider the discussion on the passages from Ephesians and 1 Corinthians.

Resources

Brueggeman, Walter, *Praying the Psalms*.
Kraybill, Donald, *The Upside-Down Kingdom*.

9

The Church as Counterculture

IT WAS MOTHER'S DAY. The visiting minister had just finished her sermon. Cathy had preached on Martha, noting her virtues. "She was a do-er. Her faith was always expressed by good works."

Cathy confessed her former tendency to denounce "Martha-types." She spoke of mothers, and how she and others mini-mized the crucial, daily acts of service that such "Marthas" per-form.

Cathy noted Martha's bold exchange with Jesus in Luke at the time of her brother Lazarus' death. Martha became the first person to confess, "You are the Messiah, the Son of God."

Cathy, a warm and engaging speaker, urged her listeners to follow Martha's example of Christ-centered faith translated into acts of loving service. The congregation responded positively. There was an upbeat spirit as the group began the closing hymn.

Cathy joined her husband and young daughter, Rachel, for the singing. At about verse two, the bowl of Cheerios Rachel held slipped from her fingers. Tiny oat circles scattered all over the rug in front of the pulpit.

Cathy immediately bent down to begin the cleanup. Others smiled and continued to sing joyfully.

Then James, the senior pastor, a man sixty years old, dressed in dark suit and tie, stepped from his place third row back. He walked forward, bent down, and gathered the wayward Cheerios.

James was a powerful witness as he stooped before the church. Like Martha, he demonstrated a willingness to share in humble tasks and to put faith to action.

Introduction

Responding to family violence includes getting the whole picture. We can observe and respond to individual cases of family violence. Yet we also must understand how the churches and our larger culture support such power abuses.

Ruth Krall (quoted in chapter 5) employs an image from her childhood. A horse with blinders trots along a highway. The blinders enable the horse to focus on the road ahead, freed from the distraction of the cars speeding alongside.

A true analysis of the full dimensions of family violence entails removing the blinders. As frightening and overwhelming as that is, our consideration of family violence leads to consideration of all the factors that set up and encourage abuse. However, we do such analysis so we can experience God's renewal. Our willingness to name the sins of family and sexual violence will lead us to healing and new life.

What are the speeding cars in our society? How do we identify and respond to them?

There are three main elements to this chapter. First we consider a Bible story and examine how Jesus set a standard for the church as counterculture. Then we consider a few "snapshots" of North American culture and compare those examples with Jesus's model. Finally we examine the local church.

A Bible Story—Jesus Responds to the Religious Leaders' Trap

In John 8:1-11, we read of Jesus's clash with the dominant culture. After a solitary night of prayer on the Mount of Olives,

Jesus, early in the morning went to the temple. As the people gathered round, he sat and began to teach them.

The religious leaders brought a woman who had been caught in adultery. Making her stand before all of them, the leaders said to Jesus, "Teacher, this woman was caught in the very act of committing adultery. Now in the law Moses commanded us to stone such women. Now what do you say?" They said this to test him, so that they might have some charge to bring against him.

Jesus bent and wrote with his finger on the ground. When they kept questioning him, he straightened up and said, "Let anyone among you who is without sin be the first to throw a stone at her." And again he bent down and wrote on the ground.

When they heard it, the leaders left, one by one, beginning with the elders. Jesus was left alone with the woman standing before him. Jesus said, "Woman, where are they? Has no one condemned you?"

She said, "No one, sir."

And Jesus said, "Neither do I condemn you. Go your way, and from now on do not sin again."

Reflections on the Bible Story

1. This story focuses on the trap. The religious leaders of the day were deliberately trying to catch Jesus.

The leaders intended to force Jesus into conflict with the dominant group—those in either religious authority or civil authority, depending on Jesus' position regarding the law of Moses. As noted in the passage, the law of Moses commanded that adulterous women be stoned to death. If Jesus affirmed such a response, he would be in trouble with the civil authorities, the Romans, who would not permit the execution.

If Jesus did not uphold the sentence, he would appear to be rejecting the law of Moses, condoning sin, and engaging in conflict with the religious leaders.

Either way he was in trouble. The leaders thought they had a sure catch.

2. Our understanding of the woman caught in adultery needs to include recognition that this was a trap. It is possible she was framed.

3. Jesus found a way out of the trap. He reframed the debate from a legal one to a moral one. He turned the sin back on the accusers. He deftly replied, "Let anyone among you who is without sin be the first to throw a stone at her." The religious leaders were caught. Each recognized his own sin, including, perhaps, sexual sin. Silenced in their accusations, the leaders departed.

4. Of course, the conflict between Jesus and the religious leaders did not end with this exchange. Jesus successfully avoided their trap. But he publicly confronted their sinfulness. They continued to clash with him. The conflicts intensified and they sought to kill Jesus.

5. We must ponder the absence of the woman's lover. Where was the man? Why is the woman brought alone? According to the law of Moses (Lev. 20:10), both the adulterer and the adulteress were to be put to death. Was there an actual act of adultery or was an innocent woman set up to serve the accusers' cause?

6. Jesus responded sensitively to the woman, empowering her. We can imagine her standing terrified, humiliated, half-naked or with her clothes in disarray. Jesus spoke directly to her, questioned her, and allowed her voice to be heard. He then made three statements. He did not condemn her. He told her to go on her way. He instructed her, "Do not sin again."

He elevated her from a fallen and condemned women to a person with a voice, freed to make choices.

Making the Bible Story Our Story

1. It is no accident that Jesus' astute response to the religious leaders' trap occurred after a night of prayer. Being centered in God is a necessary resource when confronting evil.

2. Things are not always what they seem. The religious leaders appeared to be righteous, seeking to uphold the morality of the community. Jesus' reply forced them to acknowledge their own sin.

3. Systems can be brutally unjust. The woman was roughly and publicly identified as a sexual sinner deserving of punishment. Her partner and the religious leaders had no such public exposing.

4. The church's mission is to follow Jesus' example. Recog-

nize the trap. Name the system truthfully. Free victims from unjust condemnation. Direct people away from sin.

Making the Connections

One of the most remarkable things about Jesus' response to the religious leaders in the above story is his ability to critique the system. It is difficult when one is within a system also to have the perspective to analyze the system. To do so requires a shift of perspective.

We touched on this briefly in chapter 8 in our discussion of the Levite's abuse of his concubine. The ability to see things from different points of view is required in responding to family violence. We must find ways of stepping outside of our normal perspectives to view the system accurately.

My ability to shift perspective has been aided by listening to outsiders. In my experience insiders have great difficulty in critiquing the group. Their position in the center clouds their vision. Outsiders, because of their presence on the fringe, are better able to identify the structure of the system.

At various places in my life, I discover that I am (or perceive myself to be) an insider or an outsider. I inhabit a white, female, middle-aged body. My white skin is a privilege, a status symbol that enables me to partake of some of the best that North American society offers. (I have also felt vulnerable as a white person when I attended a movie about racism, sensed the deep anger of the theater patrons, and numbered myself in the minority.)

As a woman, I know that my gifts of ministry are unwelcome in some churches because of my gender. I live with a certain degree of fear, knowing that I stand a one-in-four chance of being sexually assaulted in my lifetime. I choose not to walk my city streets alone at night because of potential attackers.

As a woman, I also know a rich, sophisticated emotional strength. I am well acquainted with my emotions and can manage them or be managed by them. As a woman, I have been privileged to have the profound experience of giving birth.

In middle-age I also know a certain power that comes from having paid my dues. Settled into church, work, and family, I enjoy support, good pay, and respect—in short, privilege.

In some ways I am inside. In others, I am outside.

As we analyze our communities and our churches let us listen to the outsiders. Much can be learned about health and abilities by listening to people who are differently-abled. Much can be learned about prejudice and tolerance by listening to minority voices—Native North Americans, African-Americans, Latinos, Francophones, Asians, immigrants, and other peoples of color. Much can be learned about family violence by listening to the stories and perspectives of survivors and repentant offenders. Much can be learned about the power imbalances of our culture by listening to those with less power.

A Collection of Snapshots

What follows is a collection of observations from my personal life. Reflection on such snapshots enables us to increase our ability to shift perspectives and deepen out our analysis of society.

1. My friend Gina told me of her struggle to feel attractive in her Chinese body, because she saw only Caucasians as public models of beauty in our society. (This took on personal meaning for me when I was pregnant and saw no pregnant bodies in the ads in the fabric store when I shopped.) Until recently, there were no regular nonwhite cartoon characters in my daily newspaper. Gina, people of color, and I could not find ourselves in the public images of our society.

The message? White is valued, people of color are discounted.

2. Suzanne was three years old. Her infant brother had just knocked over a plant at my house. She faced me, hands on hips and ordered imperiously "You clean that up!" I responded with a sharp retort before realizing that my anger was caused by the challenge to my authority.

The message? Adults give orders; children obey.

3. Julio demands that he have complete control of the finances. His wife, Marguerite, has no access to funds from the bank, turns her paycheck over to him, and requests funds from Julio whenever she needs to make purchases for herself or the children.

The message? Men have greater financial power; women have less financial power.

4. I witness and intervene in four conflicts at the neighborhood school in a six-week period. The participants, from eight to eleven years old, are all male. Each time I see tears and helpless frustration in at least one of the boys.

The message? The physical violence of our culture is oppressive to males.

5. I reluctantly read my local newspaper for a one-week period to tally anecdotal evidence. In the family violence articles, nearly all of the offenders are male. All of the survivors (if they did in fact survive) are women and children.

The message? In intimate relationships men use their power in violent ways. Women and children are the targets of men's violence.

6. I take my young son to a family show. In the movie family, the father is crotchety and distracted from his wife and children's true needs. The change comes when the father punches out the bad guy. "Wow!" exclaim the kids with awe, "you're cool, Dad." The wife purrs, "Honey, I've never seen you so attractive."

The message? Men are to use their physical power in violent ways and their loved ones will admire them for it.

7. I attended a peacemaking conference several years ago. I was buoyed by the positive attitudes of the workshop leaders. They demonstrated a sophisticated and believable approach to conflict resolution. A new world seemed possible listening to their ideas and approaches.

But the most significant thing that I carried with me was the beauty and strength of the many female leaders. They were intelligent, articulate, competent, and above all *empowered*. Leading by themselves or coleading with each other or men, they were stunning examples of what effective female leaders could look like.

How different when I flip through the pages of a weekly news magazine. The power players, all around the world, are virtually all male, nearly all middle-aged or older, dressed in identical dark suits and ties. So homogeneous!

Women in the magazines sell products or are media stars—actresses or musicians. They are mostly young and conform to our society's expectations of beauty.

The message? Our dominant culture does not offer a vision in which women and men are equal and power is shared. We must seek this model in a counterculture.

8. I'm toodling around town doing my Saturday errands. I see the small group of men at the intersection ahead. I know who they are even before I get close enough to read their placards, "Men Against Violence Against Women."

My eyes fill with tears. I gently toot the horn and wave as I pass.

"Why did you beep, Mom?" my son inquires.

"I beeped to say 'hi' to those men."

"Why did you beep? Do you know them?"

"No, I don't know them. I beeped because they are marching and I'm glad they're marching."

"Why are they marching?"

I pause, torn between preserving the innocence of a five-year-old and responding to his thirst for information. I leap. "There are men who hit their wives and children and other women. Sometimes they hurt them badly. These men marching today are saying they are against the violence. They're saying 'no way' to violence against women and children."

He digests this. "Mama, does Daddy ever hit you?"

"No, sweetheart, no," I reassure him, grieving in my heart all the mamas and the children who cannot be so quickly soothed.

The message? We can speak out against the violence in our culture and affirm relationships based on mutuality, respect, and equality.

Most anywhere we look in our culture, we observe the themes of oppression. Those with the balance of power use it in ways that are harmful. Men dominate women. Adults dominate children. Whites dominate people of color. Other vulnerable groups—the physically and mentally disabled and the elderly—are subject to oppression by the dominant groups.

In the Church

The church has the potential to offer a different perspective. In fact, the church is intended to be a counterculture. The Bible is a wonderful testament to God's invitation to create an alternative to our oppressive dominant culture. (Later in this chapter we will consider how the local church can be evaluated as to whether it sends out the messages of the dominant culture or the messages of God's counterculture.)

We must confess the church's susceptibility to the dominant culture. Our Western culture has unfortunately been exported with our missionary and economic efforts; all too often it is the worst part of our culture that gets conveyed. We must separate our North American culture from what God intends for us.

The biblical message is a counterpoint to the dominant messages of our culture. One passage from Romans is worth our consideration.

> Do not be conformed to this world [or age],
> but be transformed by the renewing of your minds,
> so that you may discern what is the will of God—
> what is good and acceptable and perfect.
>   (Romans 12:2)

Here we are being urged to avoid conforming to the dominant culture. The passage continues with specific instructions that mark the true Christian.

> Let love be genuine; hate what is evil,
> hold fast to what is good;
> love one another with mutual affection;
> outdo one another in showing honor.
>   Do not lag in zeal,
> be ardent in spirit, serve the Lord.
>   Rejoice in hope, be patient in suffering,
> persevere in prayer.
>   Contribute to the needs of the saints;
> extend hospitality to strangers.
>   Bless those who persecute you;
> bless and do not curse them.
>   Rejoice with those who rejoice,
> weep with those who weep.
>   Live in harmony with one another;
> do not be haughty, but associate with the lowly;
> do not claim to be wiser than you are.
>   Do not repay anyone evil for evil,
> but take thought for what is noble in the sight of all.

If it is possible, so far as it depends on you,
live peaceably with all.
(Romans 12:9-18)

Note how we are instructed to have compassionate, just relationships within the church. Power is to be shared, not used to
lord over others. Empathy and harmony are emphasized.

The persecution and suffering noted in the text is in reference to the attacks by government leaders on the early church.
Christians are being instructed how to respond to such assaults
by civil leaders. The attacks are not seen as being part of the intimate connections of family and church; indeed such violence
has no place among believers.

We turn again to Jesus' life to learn from his example of
shared power. He stepped outside societal boundaries with his
intimate conversation with the Samaritan woman at the well
(John 4). We see his compassion toward Martha as he responds
to her grief (John 11). We witness his acceptance of Mary's act of
discipleship as she washes Jesus' feet with her hair. (This story in
John 12 occurs just a chapter before Jesus washes his disciples'
feet.)

All of these stories depict women interacting with Jesus in
ways that suggest mutual respect and equality. This is all the
more remarkable given the context of the Bible culture, where
women had significantly less power than they do today. Although the names and stories of the male disciples have been
preserved in detail for the Christian church (suggesting the
dominance of males), it is still significant that we have these
glimpses of Jesus interacting with women. We can infer that
God's understanding of how women and men are to interact is
based on how Jesus related to women.

Jesus did not dominate or control. He treated women as real
people. He responded to their questions with sincerity and respect. In short, Jesus modeled right relationships.

Considering the Local Church

How do we analyze our local church? How do we recognize
the places where our church is truly following Jesus, and the

places where we are woefully astray, influenced by the dominant culture?

Asking questions is a good way to begin. Listed below are four general themes as well as questions to consider under those themes.

Power and Influence

1. Who is most visible in the church? How are people on the fringe encouraged to make their voices heard? How are people empowered? How are people disempowered?

2. How do decisions get made? Is the decision-making process concentrated in the hands of a few, or is the process designed to include as many voices and perspectives as possible?

3. What style of leadership is modeled by church leaders? Are they open to feedback, do they consult with others? Or are they "Lone Rangers," their use of power not questioned?

Conflict

1. Is conflict named and dealt with openly? Or does it remain underground?

2. Who decides what conflicts will be dealt with publicly and by what process? A few people? Or representatives who relate to the whole congregation?

3. Is conflict viewed as bad, with the focus being on determining who's right and wrong and who's to blame? Or is conflict seen as an opportunity to discern together God's will for a stronger church?

4. Does conflict become an opportunity for one group to control another? Or is conflict seen as a way to empower others?

5. Is asking questions encouraged or discouraged?

Male-Female Relationships

1. Who is in charge? Are both men and women given equal opportunity to share their gifts in all areas of church life?

2. Who serves? Are both men and women equally represented in behind-the-scenes ministries, like care of children, provision of food, maintenance of the church building?

3. Does the public input, through worship and Sunday

school, affirm that both females and males are created equal in the image of God?

Sexuality

1. How is human sexuality recognized in the church? Is it affirmed or discounted?

2. Are boundaries encouraged? Are children touched against their will or respected when they decline physical touch?

3. Is sex described as a wife's duty and a husband's right? Are messages given that suggest males cannot control their expressions of sexuality?

4. Are children and teenagers provided with accurate sexual information that includes Christian values?

5. Is mutual consent upheld as necessary for sexual activity?

Prayer

Dear God,

You placed us in societies as well as in families and churches. We acknowledge our society has often gone astray from your intention of just and affirming communities. We acknowledge the same straying in our church and families. Help us to right our paths and turn towards you. Amen.

Discussion Questions

1. Consider the discussion on inside/outside. Where are you an insider, with privilege and a sense of belonging? Where do you experience yourself as an outsider, feeling threatened and unconnected?

2. Share your reflections on the snapshots. Which of the vignettes match your experience? Which are unfamiliar to you?

3. How is your church participating in the dominant culture in ways that seem un-Christian?

4. How is your church offering an alternative to the dominant culture?

5. Use any of the questions about the local church to analyze your own congregation.

10

The Churches Respond

PASTOR GORDON MAXWELL pondered the woman in his office. Anita appeared believable. There were no fresh bruises or marks of assault, but the truth of her testimony sounded strong.

She described repeated physical and sexual abuse by her husband. It was horrible. Gordon knew Anita had confided in him only because of the trust that had developed in previous counseling sessions. Her revelation also signaled the seed of personal strength beginning to grow in her. He knew she needed support to leave the abusive marriage.

Gordon also saw how breaking the secret of Jack's abuse would affect others. Would Jack leave the home willingly if confronted about the abuse? Where would Anita and the children live if he did not?

How would other members of the church react? Would they find it difficult to believe the truth because of Jack's role as deacon? Would they pressure Anita to stay in the marriage, tell her to change, and avoid holding Jack responsible for his abusive actions?

Other survivors of physical and sexual violence would surely have their wounds opened. Would they identify themselves? Would the church respond compassionately?

What about other offenders? How could the congregation draw them out of their sinfulness into repentance and healthy Christian family relationships?

It all seemed so overwhelming.

At the moment, however, Anita was waiting for his response. "We are with you," Gordon told her. "I will walk with you as you seek healing from the abuse."

Introduction

The Christian church has a valuable opportunity to be a strong, healthy force helping to end family violence. People come to church for a variety of reasons. One strong attraction is hope for healing.

The survivors of family violence bear powerful witness to the pull of faith. In spite of suffering cruelty and abuse, often at the hands of other Christians, these courageous souls still turn to the Christian church hoping to find healing. Faith becomes one resource enabling them to heal. The local church can help or hinder that healing process.

This chapter consists of three parts. The first section addresses two main obstacles that block the church from effective response. The second section examines what can be done to prepare the church to open up discussion on the topic of family violence. The goal is to create an environment where all of us can name the problem. The third section looks at what a congregation can do after disclosure. It addresses steps to take when people are aware of a specific family violence situation that is current or has occurred.

Obstacles to Church Response
"I Just Want It to Go Away"

It has been suggested that talking about family violence makes it worse. "This stuff is best handled in private" is one comment. Or, "You talk about it long enough and everyone will believe they've been abused." For many people, the reality of family violence is too disturbing to acknowledge. In many places there is a backlash that threatens to drive this tragedy back into silence.

This dynamic continues to operate in our societies and will likely operate in your local church as well. However, the only way to heal from this horror is to openly acknowledge its existence, actively educate ourselves, and work to end it. Refusing to address it because of fear or denial will not make it go away. Identifying it, speaking out against it, offering treatment and healing for those affected—this is the path of recovery.

Karl is an active churchman who opened himself to reflection on family violence and sexual abuse. He was particularly dismayed by revelations of sexual abuse by church leaders. "At first I was upset with the church press," he stated. "It seemed like sensationalism. But the more I thought about it, the more I realized this sexual abuse stuff is everywhere. It's in the churches. It's in the schools. It's in families. Somehow Christians are going to have to learn to deal with it."

In every case, when church leaders begin to identify themselves as available to discuss family violence, survivors seize the opportunity to speak openly.

What If the Victim Is Lying?

We are blocked from responding effectively to family violence because of our difficulty believing the victim.

"What about when the victim is lying?" people inquire. "We all know of people who have been wrongfully accused." The concern about false accusations is regularly raised when the topic of family violence is discussed.

My response includes a number of points. First, we need to be careful not to continue our tending automatically to disbelieve victims. Church and society do need just and orderly procedures for ensuring the truth of charges, but such procedures must not be biased in the direction of discounting victim's stories.

We hold a cherished belief that the nuclear family is a good and stable unit, providing all the emotional needs required by family members. To retain our belief in the security of the nuclear family, we deny the reality of victims' pain. In summary, the very fact that we have disbelieved for so long is one reason we must currently start with believing the victim (while remaining open to contradictory data if it appears).

Second, it is important to be aware of how few cases of false accusation actually exist. Most people do not make up stories of physical or sexual abuse. The experience of being labeled a victim as well as the disbelief, rejection, and ridicule that victims experience are too negative to be worth making up a story.

If the story includes falsities (which does happen occasionally, particularly with children and adolescents), they generally relate to some details of the abuse which may be blurred or confused. Or the victim may falsely name an offender. The victim likely has been abused but is not able correctly to identify the offender. Again remember that these are a minority of cases.

Third, it is important to remember our biases. Peter Rutter (*Sex in the Forbidden Zone*, pp. 9-13) discusses his biases as he writes about sexual abuse by professionals. He identified with the offenders because of characteristics he shared with them— male, professional, helper. He wrestled with the internal dilemma of seeing himself as like the offender and wanting to absolve the offender's guilt while simultaneously recognizing the truth of the victim's experience. His dilemma was resolved only when he accepted the survivor's story while acknowledging the depth of his identification with the offender. We are similarly challenged to recognize our biases.

For example, we have been trained to disbelieve children. Lacking the language and concepts of adults, their stories often seem like nonsense to adults. Our stories were similarly dismissed when we were children.

Deception, or the blurring of fantasy with reality, is characteristic of some children at some ages. Still a general principle to affirm is that there is a kernel of truth embedded in most of what children communicate to us.

A second example concerns our biases about men and women. These stereotypes get in the way of truly listening. We often have difficulty accepting men as weak or hurting. When Renee's husband was dying from unsuccessful heart surgery, the nurses remarked to Renee that he was acting "just like a man, not able to handle the pain." This tendency not to express pain makes it difficult for men to voice their experiences of being physical and sexual abuse victims.

Another example relates to women's sexuality. Women are portrayed as possessing enormous sexual powers. They are seen as seductive and tempting, overpowering men. This myth leads to ridiculous and tragic scenarios.

A judge, in ruling a father innocent on a charge of sexually molesting his infant daughter, included a comment that the "seductiveness" of the infant "caused" the father's assault.

In the public media, women are consistently portrayed in highly sexualized ways. This falsehood contributes to a misunderstanding of women's sexuality and also suggests that women's sexuality is responsible for men's sexual abuses.

Believing the victim requires that we acknowledge the denial, the misperceptions, and the biases that accompany discussions of family violence.

Church leaders must exercise sensitivity when dealing with a situation where one person has identified abuse and the alleged offender denies the abuse. Church leaders must take an unambiguous stand against the abuse of power and work to provide opportunities for the truth to become clear.

Preparation

The local church provides an excellent setting in which to discuss family violence. Individuals or subgroups can open up the subject in a variety of ways.

Consider the following educational formats.

1. Family violence can be addressed in a sermon or a series of sermons. This can happen in Sunday morning worship or at another service time. A survivor or repentant offender can be invited to share from personal experience during the sermon time.

2. Children's time can be used to educate children both about family violence and sexual abuse. In addition to a number of how-to books, there are gentle story books that instruct (see Resources).

3. Sunday school classes for all ages are another effective for-

mat. Adults, teenagers, and children can learn about and discuss the topic. One class of teenagers used role-plays to explore responses to sexual harassment (see Resources).

4. Library resources can be included which address family violence. These resources can be publicized through the church newsletter or other vehicles (see Resources).

5. A special event, for a subgroup or the entire church, can be held. An outside resource person, such as a professional counselor, a representative from the local women's shelter, or a person directly involved in abuse—survivor, recovering offender, or family member—could speak. A film or video could be shown. Afterward break up into small groups for more open discussion.

6. Publicize community resources, like groups for violent men, self-help groups for survivors, and women's shelters. Support these groups by including them in your budget and through fundraising projects.

7. Encourage church leaders to become educated so that they can note warning signs and follow up on their concerns with caring, open interest (see Resources).

8. Develop a policy or process. Most churches have no idea how to respond to a family violence situation. Contact your conference district office for suggestions. The lack of preparation means that valuable time and energy is directed toward policy development at the time of disclosure, when family and other church members are most in need of pastoral care. As in other crises, if advance preparation has occurred, everyone will be in a better position to respond.

Consider the following questions.

1. If a member discloses family violence that is current, what individual leader or group responds to the violence? If a child is the victim or at risk, who will report this to the legal authorities?

2. What referrals and supports are offered to family members?

3. How is the abuse identified to the congregation?

4. Who makes decisions about the offender's sin, repentance, treatment, and restoration to fellowship?

Determine clear policy on these questions. Publicize it to the congregation so that everyone knows the policy to be followed.

When the Secret Is Told

Given the current statistics on family violence (quoted in this book and elsewhere), there is a good chance families in your church are struggling with physical, sexual and/or emotional abuse. When the secret becomes public, the sisters and brothers of the church family have a precious opportunity to respond. The following steps offer concrete suggestions for such response.

You may become aware of adult survivors of childhood abuse. The healing from the abuse is current even if the abuse is not. While the focus in this section is on current cases of abuse, much of the material can be applied to survivors of past abuse.

Justice-Making

The abuse of power is an injustice. The church as it responds to family violence has the job of making justice. (This concept of justice-making has been developed by Marie M. Fortune and is articulated by her in a number of her writings.)

Justice-making begins with truth-telling. It continues with confronting the offender. For perfect justice to occur, the offender responds by admitting guilt, acknowledging the harm caused by the abuse, expressing remorse, and seeking repentance. Offenders can further attempt to make justice by offering restitution to their victims. (Restitution means making payment for damages done. It is a concrete act by the offender which symbolizes the repentance of the offender.)

Healing may occur after these steps of justice-making have happened. So may forgiveness and reconciliation. However, healing, forgiveness, and reconciliation may not follow.

It is rare that the offender follows through on the necessary steps. But the survivor's healing is not dependent on the offender's response. The church can be an extremely helpful resource to survivors. As Fortune writes in *Violence in the Family*, "Justice-making for a victim breaks through her isolation, affirms for her that what she has experienced is wrong and not her fault, and affirms this on behalf of the whole community" (p. 184).

Believe the Victim

Support the victim in breaking the silence. Offer victims every support you can to assist them in identifying the abuse.

Your willingness to believe the victim is one of the most significant roles you can take. The victim moves to survivor as a witness believes the story of the abuse and assists in the healing.

Community Resources

The family in your church will likely become quickly involved with a number of community agencies, either voluntarily or by order of the court. The sheer number and unfamiliarity of the agencies can be distressing for each member of the family.

If the abuse involves a child, notify the local child protection agency (Family and Children Services or Child Welfare Agency). In many places in North America, any individual who suspects that a child is being abused is required by law to report that information to the child protection agency.

The child protection agency is designed to make the child's needs a priority. The intent is that specially trained people become involved to investigate the abuse, implement healing supports for the child, and develop treatment plans for the abuser(s). Some families experience this agency as helpful. Others do not.

Counseling may not be required by law, but it is a potentially vital part of the healing. The counseling profession has more expertise in this field than does any other profession. Counselors can assist survivors in healing and offenders in stopping the abuse. Counselors, or professionals with training in the area of family violence, can also provide valuable educational information.

The criminal justice system may also be involved with families who have abusive patterns. One church discovered the local court system to be extremely responsive to the church's input. Possible involvements include these: write a letter to the judge to describe the church's involvement with the offender and the family and the church's commitment to stopping family violence; avoid providing character witnesses for offenders who are trying to manipulate the courts; offer input into the presentencing report and the sentencing; take an active role in the community service order.

Supporting the Family

Treat a family abuse crisis as you would any other crisis. Offer practical as well as emotional support. Offer to pay for counseling for family members. Arrange childcare for an individual who is suddenly a single parent.

It is preferable that children and the nonoffending spouse remain in the family home if their safety can be assured. Offer alternate accommodation to the offender. If the offender is not out of the home, offer accommodation to other family members so they have a safe, comfortable alternative to living with the abuser.

Provide a neutral, observant atmosphere where an abusive parent can visit children.

Offer meals, remember birthdays, and in other ways assist in the family's needs for happy, sociable times.

Support victims in doing whatever is necessary to stop the abuse. Recognize that abuse harms families. It may be impossible or dangerous for families to remain in or return to an intact state.

Form special support groups around the family members—one for the offender, one for the nonoffending spouse, one for the victim, if appropriate. These groups should be composed of trusted church leaders who are spiritually mature, good listeners, and sensible.

While not therapy groups, the groups will have therapeutic effects, assist the adults in making healthy decisions, and help to shoulder the pain and brokenness resulting from the abuse.

Caring for the Offender

Consider these verses from Galatians 1:6-2:

> My friends, if anyone is detected in a transgression, you who have received the Spirit should restore such a one in a spirit of gentleness.
> Take care that you yourselves are not tempted.

> Bear one another's burdens, and in this way you will fulfill the law of Christ.

This passage offers a number of guidelines as we attempt the challenge of setting the correct path in response to an offender.

1. Our goal is to *restore* the sinner in a spirit of gentleness. This involves a disciplined, firm, compassionate approach.

2. Church leaders must guard against falling prey to similar sins. While we are dealing with another's fallenness, we cannot forget our own tendency to abuse power.

3. Finally, we take on each other's burdens in response to Christ taking on ours. As members of one family, we share each other's sufferings.

In responding to the offender, it is crucial to recognize that the offender will require intense therapy to overcome the abusive tendencies. Insist on professional treatment; offer to assist with payment. Be realistic about the offender's tendency to abuse. Avoid allowing the offender to be in vulnerable positions. (For example, don't allow a child molester to teach Sunday school to youngsters.)

Offer the offender friendship. Many offenders are desperately lonely and insecure people. When their abusive behavior becomes public, they may lose all or most of their network—regular contact with family, work acquaintances, and friends. Remember their social needs.

Provide the offender with a place to sort out spiritual issues of sin, guilt, repentance, and forgiveness.

Process the Congregational Pain

Abuse hurts and the knowledge that a church family has suffered abuse hurts the whole church. Each congregation will respond differently, and the leadership group must determine what response fits their particular church.

Designate a group responsible to devise and oversee the processing needed by the congregation. This is not a one-person job. Three or four people should be given the task to discern God's leading, respond to those most affected, and set and implement a variety of steps.

Keep the following in mind:

1. Church leaders must declare themselves firmly opposed to family violence.

2. Invite other survivors and offenders to declare themselves and offer them support and resources.

3. Provide clear, direct information to the people it concerns most. Offer opportunities for people to talk safely, ask questions, explore their thoughts and emotions, be educated. Recognize that people do not like to address the pain of family violence. Expect to encounter resistance, denial, and obstructions.

4. Ask a professional to lead an information meeting.

5. Consider a time for the offender to tell his or her story to the congregation as a part of the healing process for everyone. Allow opportunity for the congregation to ask questions and voice concerns or support to the offender.

6. Recognize that survivors (of the particular offender as well as survivors of other offenders) will likely have an extremely painful reaction to the presence of the offender. The current offender will symbolize *their* offender, and many survivors will associate the same intense feelings of panic and anger with the current offender.

This is a necessary and difficult reality. Survivors cannot be pushed into accepting the offender "as a Christian brother" or "forgiving in Christian love." Survivors can be listened to, accepted, and given permission to voice their feelings.

7. The offender may have been disciplined by the church and may not be a full member of the congregation. When the offender has demonstrated admission of guilt, acknowledgement of harm, remorse and repentance, and offered restitution, arrange (if appropriate) for restoration to fellowship.

This could take the form of a binding-and-loosing service. The offender gathers with members of the congregation or church leaders who bind the offender from participating in certain activities where the offender is vulnerable to sin (such as youth ministry) and loose the offender into other church activities (such as regular participation in public worship). Such a service marks the process of brokenness and restoration for all.

8. Above all, guard against premature reconciliation or easy

forgiveness (see chapter 11 for a discussion of forgiveness and reconciliation).

Summary

The faithful church will respond actively to family violence. It has been said that the church must manage the conflict or the conflict will manage the church. The same is true for conflict involving family violence.

Prepare yourselves for a long, complex, wearying process (a minimum of two years). Know that truth-telling, justice-making, support, and God's gracious love hold the keys for healing.

Prayer

Dear God,

You call us to stand with suffering and heal the brokenhearted. Empower us to deal compassionately and carefully with the family violence which exists in our church families. Amen.

Discussion Questions

1. Reflect on the difficulty of responding to family violence. Discuss your own wish that it would just go away.

2. Discuss the information about wrongful accusations. Offer any stories or insights you may have. Be sensitive to survivors who may be present.

3. What policy, if any, is in place in your congregation? How do people get informed of the policy? Who is responsible for setting up and updating the policy? If you do not have a policy, who can be encouraged to develop one?

4. What steps would you like to see your congregation take in responding to family violence?

5. Consider the discussion on justice-making. Share stories of injustices and justice-making. How was the church involved or absent in these examples?

Resources

Fortune, Marie M., *Violence in the Family*.
Reid, Kathryn Goering with Marie M. Fortune, *Preventing Child Sexual Abuse: A Curriculum for Children Ages 9-12*.
Rutter, Peter, *Sex in the Forbidden Zone*.

11

What to Do When There's Nothing to Do

MARCELLA LOVED her church. She was grateful for the way God had redeemed her life, blessing her with a steady husband and two beautiful children. Gradually God was healing her of the wounds of her abusive childhood and the self-abuse of her turbulent adolescence.

As a pastor's wife, she received opportunities to minister to many hurting people. Sensing Marcella's willingness to listen and her compassion that acted as a balm on the raw places, women sought her out.

As an incest survivor, Marcella was tuned to pick up and respond to other sexual abuse survivors. So she was the first to know Alice's sad story. Alice, now with children of her own, and her father, Charlie, were both members of St. John's Church, where Marcella and her husband, Devon, ministered.

Marcella and Devon worked with the situation sensitively and carefully. Alice was given support and encouragement. Eventually Charlie was confronted by Alice with Marcella and Devon present. He denied it and steadfastly maintained his innocence.

Alice reported that she felt doubly victimized—once by the initial abuse and secondly by her father's denial. Church members split, with some supporting Alice and others believing Charlie. Marcella and Devon agonized over their broken flock. They knew Alice's abuse had not been acknowledged, yet they didn't know what to do next.

Introduction

Many people in many churches across the land are finding themselves in the same situation as Marcella and Devon. Good intentions, careful planning, and a sincere commitment to justice-making bump against resistance and denial. The good work grinds to a halt.

In the words of the writer of Ecclesiastes, "I saw all the oppressions that are practiced under the sun. Look, the tears of the oppressed—with no one to comfort them! On the side of their oppressors there was power—with no one to comfort them" (4:1).

How do we respond when we are stuck? At points, recovering from the tragedy of family violence seems as possible as moving a mountain. All our best efforts—spiritual discernment, moral outrage, sensitive planning—crash against the immense weight of rocklike resistance.

Much of the Christian tradition is useful in this regard. For even mountains can be worn away through the persistent efforts of wind and water (compare the Rockies to the Appalachians or the Gatineaus). And the Bible and Christian tradition offer us models of what to do when it appears there is nothing to do.

Accept the Enormity of the Task

Recovering from family violence is an immense task. Thousands of people have been traumatized; there have been centuries of oppression and silence; and too often society still ignores family violence. Such problems will not go away overnight.

In fact, we are discussing a values shift, which takes a minimum of a generation, or twenty-five to thirty years. Some writers use the term *paradigm shift*. This occurs when our core assumptions are altered, either gradually over time or through a significant challenging event. Consider these two examples.

1. Jay was putting out the garbage one morning. His three-year-old daughter, Michelle, offered to help, "Let's take out the garbage, Daddy."

"We'll put it out for the garbage man to collect," Jay added.

"Garbage man?" Michelle questioned. "Can't women be garbage collectors too? Can't I be a garbage collector when I grow up?"

"Of course, honey," Jay quickly responded, anxious to encourage his daughter's confidence in her choices. "Women can do anything they want."

2. I sat recently with family friends. Adults and children were telling school stories. I told of being swatted by the teacher when I was in second grade. My hat was snatched by a classmate while we were sitting at the lunch table. I retrieved it, the teacher saw only my action, and I got the punishment.

Chris told of Grandma getting her hand smacked for misspelling a word. Grandma Ruth was probably as sweet and pleasant then as she is now, and the punishment seemed severe.

The children listened to the stories and smiled. Maybe they were imagining the adults as children, laughing about them being in trouble. Maybe they were glad they can go to school without the fear of physical punishment. "Times have changed," an adult declared.

These examples testify to paradigm shifts. The first one marks a shift from garbage man to garbage collector, language which indicates that women are moving into jobs previously held only by men. The second example marks a shift from physical punishment as the norm in school to physical punishment as unacceptable.

Such shifts are disconcerting. We can be so unsettled that we resist the shifts and try to maintain the old ways. However, a similar paradigm shift is occurring in the public understanding of family relationships and in the relationships of men and women. The shift is away from a structure which unfairly distributes power, giving more to men and adults, less to women and children. The shift is toward a structure which values each individual equally and seeks mutual sharing of power. This shift draws from the historic consensus models developed by native North Americans, the Quakers, and others, and will serve us well as we attempt to end family abuse.

Given that we are experiencing a paradigm shift—as individuals, as a society, as churches—it is useful to recognize the enormity and complexity of the task.

Recognize that the Journey Is Ongoing

A first step is to know that the story has not ended. When you are in the midst of a difficult situation, this can be hard to imagine. However, over time things change.

Survivors grow stronger. Offenders hear confrontations, which say no to power abuses and make it more difficult for future offenses to occur. God continues to move in our hearts, inviting us into a life of wholeness.

Set Reasonable Goals

Many survivors of family violence have recognized the significance of carefully setting goals. The goals need to be not only reasonable but achievable.

For example, Mehta may want Ravi to accept responsibility for his violence and anger mismanagement. It is certainly reasonable to expect that of an offender. However, currently most offenders do not readily accept responsibility for their offenses. It is unlikely that Ravi will accept the responsibility, particularly initially.

Mehta does not want her healing to depend on Ravi's choices. She then frames her goal so she can control the outcome. She may state her goal as intending to hold Ravi responsible for the violence (as opposed to blaming herself or excusing him because of work stress). Or she may state her goal as intending to state to Ravi that she sees him as responsible for the abuses. Her statement to him does not depend on his accepting the truth of her viewpoint.

Church members working to end family violence can be similarly oriented. Setting reasonable, achievable goals can improve the possibility of success.

Question the Success Criteria

Having offered a suggestion for how to improve the chances for success, I now want to challenge the success criteria.

Church people around the world describe North American Christians as too success-oriented. Many Christians live in countries where they are persecuted and killed for their faith. They know poverty, unsanitary water and health conditions, and too much about children dying. They remind us that God's presence is with us whether or not we are successful.

Christ calls us not to success but to obedience. We are to be faithful in speaking out against injustice and oppression, even if our witness bears no immediate fruit of results. We are called to be compassionate, even if those wounded by family violence appear to be unresponsive. This is one more way of saying, "Keep track of the big picture."

Respect the Source of Your Spiritual Strength

It is crucial to maintain our life-sustaining connection to God when journeying through stormy waters.

I once heard Dorothy, a development speaker, tell of her work in a country where oppression and torture were rampant, sanctioned by the ruling power. I felt my shoulders bend down as she described the complex web that encircled the country's poor and dispossessed. Yet as she spoke, she exuded calmness and even joy. Her skin glowed, her eyes were bright, and she seemed at peace.

During the question period, I struggled to reconcile her apparent composure with the brutality she so vividly recalled. "How did you survive?" I asked her. "How did you keep it together when confronted with such horror?"

She smiled. "We [including the other workers] learned the importance of prayer. Prayer and Bible study became our daily bread. We found we had to regularly dig deeply into those disciplines to survive."

Her witnessing words return to me as I work to end oppression and address power imbalances here in my native North America.

Through meditation on the Scriptures, we encounter a broken and struggling people who sought and discovered God's liberating love in their daily lives. Hagar, the abused slave woman, was empowered to name God, whom she called, "The one who sees." The psalmist expresses our fury and despair when we encounter the abuse of the innocents. The Psalmist also voices our misery as we name our own sinfulness. Jesus gently and radically reminds us over and over that God invites us into an upside-down kingdom. There the last shall be first, the hungry shall be fed, and each of us must push through racial, cultural, and gender barriers to touch the divine in all people.

Even so, for many people the Scriptures are not a solace. They cannot find themselves in the Bible stories, and they experience anger and sadness when they attempt to do so.

We must not condemn such responses, but listen patiently. We can encourage such people and learn from them as they seek other ways to experience God's presence.

When there is nothing else we can do, we can always pray. When we do not have words to pray, we can sit silently and allow the Spirit to groan on our behalf. We can bike a country trail or drink in the gentle splash of a city park fountain to hear God's comforting presence through nature. When we are angry at injustice, even too angry to want to speak to God, we can turn our hearts to God just to passionately cry out, "I don't want to talk to you!"

The simplest acts of our faith journey—prayer and reflection on the Bible and God's word—preserve us.

The Ministry of Presence

When we are searching for something to do, we often overlook the significance of the ministry of presence. Yet the very fact that we are willing to listen and to stand alongside of suffering people is an empowering action.

As Teresa of Avila declares,

Christ has no body now on earth but yours.
Yours are the only hands with which he can do his work,
Yours are the only feet with which he can go about the world,
Yours are the only eyes through which his compassion can

shine forth upon a troubled world.
Christ has no body now on earth but yours.

The fact of our presence—our living, breathing, loving bodies—becomes essential to all those affected by family violence.

The story is told of a young child frightened by the summer thunderstorms that crashed in the night. His parents patiently explained that God was always with him; they suggested he count the seconds between the time he saw the lightning and when he heard the thunder. The parents hoped these tools would aid him in mastering his fear. A few nights later the parents were awakened by a crack of thunder. They heard their son coming down the hall to their room.

"I'm scared," he said.

"Don't you remember that God is always with you?" his mother prompted.

"Yes, but I want God with skin on," the boy replied as he burrowed under the covers with them.

Our acting as God-with-skin-on is a tangible symbol of the ever-present God whose steadfast love endures forever.

The ministry of presence is important to those to whom we minister. It is also important to us—the ministers. For when we pause from our ceaseless activity and calm our restless spirits, we encounter the divine in silence and stillness.

My local congregation was blessed with an angel in our midst for nearly six years. Lauren was a powerful testimony of God's presence in weakness. Her body was so damaged at birth that she could not move, see, hear, or speak. Her caregivers patiently taught her to suck, but through repeated illnesses she lost even that ability.

Yet anyone who held her or paused to listen to Lauren heard the heartbeat of God. We felt deep emotions—the precious value of each spark of life, the frailty of human beings, the power of touch in forging human bonds.

We suffered as she struggled for life. We agonized with and admired the family members who met the demands of her care. We wept together when she slipped from this life to the next in a blazing fever. We are grateful for the lessons about the ministry of presence provided by Lauren's short sojourn among us.

Empower Survivors

The empowering of survivors is vital for our corporate healing from family violence. As those who bear the direct scars of the abuse, they are the strongest moral force to challenge the abuse of power.

Anything we can do to empower the victim aids this process. This includes the following:

- listening to and believing the survivor's story
- accepting the emotions that accompany the abuse
- encouraging the survivor to develop and follow inner instincts
- involving the survivor in teaching others about power abuses in the family.

Converting the Offender

We must offer the opportunity for the offender to convert, to turn from old abusive patterns and toward new healthy uses of power. A repentant offender can be a particularly compelling force in the ending of family violence.

Because males are most frequently the offenders, men in particular have an invaluable opportunity to respond to and care for the offender. Converting the offenders includes:

- firm confrontation regarding the offenses
- expecting the offender to turn away from the abuse of power
- offering the offender the opportunity to acknowledge the harm caused by the abuse and make restitution as a way of responding to the survivor's need to heal and the offender's need to recover
- sensitive therapy which allows the offender the safety to explore and heal inner hurts
- demonstrating healthy models of relationships in which power is shared
- willingness to look beyond the label of offender to see a precious child of God.

Maintain Balance

Jesus sought solitude and prayer as a means of restoring his depleted resources. Caring for ourselves as we care for others is essential. I have known this in my head for many years. I continue to experience it on a deeper intuitive level with each step that I take into the abyss of family violence. When surrounded by horrific evil, we are wise to prepare ourselves to be as strong and healthy as possible.

The caregiver who sacrifices sleep, reflective time, and good eating and fitness habits will discover few reserves to draw on when the battle is engaged.

Nurture yourself. Cover the basics like sufficient rest and healthy nutrition. Balance doing with being, caregiving with replenishing resources.

Actively seek to restore the imbalance created by the necessary attending to pain and violence. Soak in a sunset. Play. Laugh. Savor music. Delight in the pleasure of human companionship.

I have been blessed during the writing of this book to have the companionship of three wonderful children. They regularly interrupt me with the rhythms of their lives. They draw my attention to a number of marvels—the grace and strength of their bodies at play, the apple tree slowly shedding its leaves, the necessity of honoring the first snowfall with snowball throws, the amazing daily spurt of the amaryllis plant, the sensuousness of bare toes on spring grass. Their joy and pleasure help restore my soul.

Your capacity to care for yourself when there is seemingly nothing to do is in fact an important action. Your ability to nourish yourself, to set limits, and to respond to pleasure is a significant statement to all those bruised by family violence. Health is possible. Nurture is a reality. Joy is in reach.

The principle of balance is as important for a church as for an individual. Church leaders need to offer opportunities for play, laughter, joy and restorative calm even as they challenge the group to deal with family power abuses effectively and firmly.

Prayer

Dear God,

There are times we feel stymied in our attempts to confront and stop family violence. There is so much pain. And the oppressors, with power on their side, refuse to repent.

Strengthen us, O God, that we may not grow weary in doing good. Instruct us in the constancy of your love. Gently enfold us in the pleasure of living. Amen.

Discussion Questions

1. Consider the discussion of paradigm shift. What paradigm shifts have you observed in your society or church or experienced personally? How do you respond to such shifts?

2. How do you keep yourself going in times of difficulty? What are your resources? What maxims do you say to yourself to encourage and motivate you?

3. Consider the comments on success. What pressures to succeed are a burden for you? How do you let go of having to be successful?

4. What is the source of your spiritual strength? What sustains you?

5. In what ways are you open to being Christ, to being his body, hands, feet, eyes in response to those hurt by the abuse of power?

12

Forgiveness and Reconciliation

Victoria strained in her seat to hear the pastor's words. His text from the Lord's Prayer (Matt. 6) centered on "Forgive us our debts, as we also have forgiven our debtors."

The word "forgive" was a trigger for Victoria's memories of her offender, her father. She described him as "someone who couldn't see a female without trying to have intercourse with her." That included her, her four sisters, her teenaged friends. She was overcome by the disgust and anger that accompanied thoughts of her father.

Taking a deep breath to steady herself she prayed, "Dear God, I am seeking guidance and healing. Please guide me and heal me." She focused on the pastor standing in the pulpit. "We don't really have a choice about forgiving," he said. "Jesus' prayer *assumes* we have forgiven, and asks God to forgive us, as we have forgiven others."

Victoria slid back into her personal thoughts. "No choice? That's certainly how I felt about my father and his forcing sex on me. I had no choice. Is this your only message for me today,

God? I cannot forgive him. Does that mean I am outside of your forgiveness?"

Introduction

Forgiveness. Reconciliation. Important concepts and experiences in our Christian walk. And difficult areas for those who have suffered violence at the hands of family members.

Forgiveness is a regular part of our corporate worship. In liturgy, hymn, prayer, Scripture, and sermon, we are reminded of and called to participate in God's forgiveness of us. We confess our sins and receive assurance of pardon. We are urged to follow Jesus who asked God to forgive his offenders.

Our human journey is guided by our understanding of how Jesus lived. When we are violated, we experience anger and bitterness. We struggle with letting go of hurts and forgiving. The more extreme the offense, the deeper the wound, the more difficulty we have in praying with Jesus, "Father, forgive them for they know not what they do."

Reconciliation is an equally significant Christian concept. In 2 Corinthians 5:18-19, Paul writes,

> God . . . reconciled us to himself through Christ, and gave us the ministry of reconciliation; that is, in Christ God was reconciling the world to himself, not counting their trespasses against them, and entrusting the message to us.

We experience reconciliation with God and yearn for that in our human relationships, particularly when those relationships have been fractured by conflict.

Myths to Consider

But we need to rethink our understandings of forgiveness and reconciliation. For some of our misunderstandings clutter the path to healing. Let's consider some commonly held myths.

Myth 1. *Forgiving means forgetting.*

But the survivors of domestic violence testify to the permanence of the effect of such violence. Healing is available—and it comes by remembering the offense, not by forgetting.

Myth 2. *Forgiving means accepting the offense.*

But the wrongs can never be justified or acceptable. All forms of abuse—physical, emotional, and sexual—have no place in any family.

Myth 3. *Forgiving is automatic.*

But our first tendency as humans is to respond to violence with violence. If you hurt me, I want to hurt you back. Reflection is often required before we relinquish that instinctual urge to inflict pain in response to injury.

Myth 4. *Forgiving is quick and a one-time event.*

But most people experience forgiveness as a process. It may occur quickly for a few individuals. However, generally it occurs over a longer period of time.

Myth 5. *Forgiving means the relationship is reconciled.*

But forgiveness is different from reconciliation. Forgiveness means the survivor has been able to let go of the resentment. It does not mean that the relationship is reconcilable, that the parent-child union can be restored, that the marriage can be resumed.

If we set aside these myths, what understandings can guide us? Let's consider definitions of forgiveness and reconciliation, reflect on a Bible story, and then rework the myths.

Definitions

To forgive is defined by *Webster's Dictionary* as—

1. To cease to feel resentment against (an offender)
2. To give up resentment of or claim to requital for (as in forgive an insult)
3. To grant relief from payment of (as in forgive a debt).

To reconcile is defined by the same source as—

1. To restore to friendship or harmony
2. To settle or resolve (differences)
3. To cause to submit to or accept (as in reconciled to hardship).

Pause for a moment over these definitions. Is "to give up resentment of" what some survivors experience when they let go of the hurt? Is being "reconciled to hardship" what some survivors mean when they accept that the abuse will always be a part of them?

Dictionary definitions act as useful starting points. We are also immensely enriched by listening to the experiences of people directly involved in family violence.

For example, one survivor wrestled with forgiveness in her healing from child sexual abuse. "What does the Bible really say?" she wondered. She set out to discover. She looked up every reference to forgiveness in the New Testament, then turned to a Greek dictionary to look up the Greek words used in the New Testament text. She noted the meaning of each Greek word and places the same word was used in other parts of the New Testament.

At the end of her meticulous labor, she concluded that one of the main meanings of the Greek word that gets translated into English as "forgive" is "to leave."

"I can do that," she declared. "I can learn 'to leave' my offender." She meant she could learn to walk past her offender without being overwhelmed by churning emotions of fear and rage.

Reconciliation, too, requires careful reflection. Reconciliation does not mean continuing the old pattern, in which the offender who previously held the balance of power abused the victim who was vulnerable to such abuses.

Reconciliation is making new relationships on new terms. Reconciliation means the victim becomes less vulnerable, more powerful. The offender becomes more careful in the use of power and seeks to empower rather than control others. For reconciliation to occur, both persons must use their power in mutually affirming ways.

A Bible Story—Joseph Forgave His Brothers

Joseph's response to the abuse of his brothers (Gen. 37, 42, 45) deserves reflection. Joseph became a victim of family violence when his brothers sold him into slavery. They showed Joseph's bloodstained robe to their father to make him believe Joseph was killed by a wild animal.

Joseph was taken to Egypt, where he gradually moved out of

slavery into a high position in government. There was a famine in the land and Joseph directed the administration of food. He was so successful that Egypt not only had enough to feed its people but to sell to neighboring countries.

Joseph's brothers, suffering from the famine, journeyed to Egypt to buy food, unknowingly, from their brother. Joseph immediately recognized them but did not identify himself. He did not forgive them or become reconciled to them. Instead he set up a series of encounters to test them.

Joseph only expressed complete reconciliation with his brothers after Judah, portrayed as the main offender, demonstrated he was a changed man, willing to lay down his life that others might live. Finally Joseph invited his brothers to bring their father, their wives, and their children to Egypt so that the whole family could live out the famine under his protection.

Reflections on the Bible Story

1. Joseph demonstrated one important facet of forgiveness and reconciliation: it is a process.

2. Joseph set in motion a series of encounters—apparently to determine if and how his brothers had changed. Were they truthful? Would they display integrity? Could he trust them?

3. The power dynamics shifted. Joseph moved from being a victim of his brothers' abuse of power toward a position of power over his brothers. From that power position, he chose to act mercifully.

4. Judah proved his conversion when he voiced his willingness to suffer for others. At that point Joseph knew that Judah had turned from the abuse of power.

In the middle of this story about Joseph and his brothers is another story about Judah (see Gen. 38). Judah betrayed the trust of his daughter-in-law Tamar. Tamar trapped Judah into confessing his mistreatment of her. He acknowledged his guilt and made restitution. Perhaps his experiences with Tamar helped Judah repent of his abuse of Joseph and turned him toward compassion and empathy.

5. Joseph declared that he had experienced God's grace in spite of his brothers' malicious actions. "God sent me before you

[to Egypt] to preserve for you a remnant on earth, and to keep alive for you many survivors" (Gen. 45:7).

Making the Bible Story Our Story

1. We too benefit from recognizing that forgiveness and reconciliation is a process that cannot be rushed or predicted.

2. The offender's response is important in the process. Offenders are called, like Judah, to acknowledge wrongdoing, make restitution, and change their abusive ways. Survivors like Joseph yearn for their offenders to show repentance.

3. Offenders need to demonstrate their changed ways over a period of time.

4. The power imbalance present when the abuse occurred must be altered. Survivors need to feel empowered, strengthened, so they can negotiate new relationships with offenders on new terms. Joseph gained power in part because of his gift of dream interpretation. Survivors need the help of the church community to heal their wounds and to move from the overwhelming sense of vulnerability toward a sense of empowerment.

5. Many survivors testify to the miracle of God's grace in spite of the abuse. Like Joseph, they are helping to keep the church alive. They not only survive the abuse but become a source of life and protection for others in the church.

Reworking the Myths

By reworking the myths with our biblical story as background, we construct some principles for helpful understandings of forgiveness and reconciliation.

1. *We acknowledge that remembering is essential for forgiveness.*

The catchy phrase "forgive and forget" is not based on reality. Perhaps it is based on our discomfort with pain, our difficulty acknowledging the emotions of anger and hatred, and the denial that is a common response to great injustice. Too often survivors are silenced with the remark, "Forgive and forget," which actually says the speaker is unwilling to listen to the survivor.

Those of us who wish to be helpful must examine our own

motives for hurrying through the excruciating process of recovery. We must learn to stay with pain. "Forgive and forget" is never appropriate counsel for survivors of family violence. Their healing depends on remembering. We must support survivors as they learn to live with the memories of their experiences.

Offenders too must remember. Their recovery is dependent on their being willing to recall and take responsibility for their actions, and recognize the effect of their abuse on their victims.

2. *We acknowledge that naming the abuse as sinful and unacceptable is essential to forgiveness.*

The survivor must acknowledge that she has been injured before she can let go of the resentment she experiences in relationship to that offense.

As witnesses, we must state our conviction that the abuse of power is unacceptable in Christian families. We must hold out a distinction between forgiveness and accepting or justifying the offense.

3. *We acknowledge that anger, hatred, and bitterness follow naturally from the abuse of power in family relationships.* Survivors have a right to experience such feelings and a right to express their pain. We place responsibility for the violation on the offender.

4. *We acknowledge that forgiveness is a process.*

Healing is a lengthy process and forgiveness, also a lengthy process, is only one part of the healing. (Reflect on the "Cycle of Relationships" at the end of the chapter.)

Trust is a necessary ingredient in relationships. When we trust we experience harmony, balance, and reconciliation.

Injury also occurs in relationship. As used here, there are two meanings of injury. One is the inevitable brokenness that we experience in relationships. We feel misunderstood, wronged, wounded. In abusive relationships, injury means violation and betrayal.

When we have been hurt, we *withdraw*. This is an instinctive response to pain, like when we pull our foot back after stubbing our toe. We withdraw from the person who has hurt us and into ourselves. We reflect on the current injury and also consider other hurts in our lives.

Such reflection leads to *healing*. We feel stronger inside and become able to turn our focus outward again.

From this strengthened self, we are better able to take risks. We have options. Some risks feel safe, while others seem too dangerous. The wisest course is to consider carefully what level of risk to take.

If we experience *acceptance*, we are able to move in the relationship back to a place of *trust*. Acceptance means, at a minimum, the other person's willingness to listen to our experience. It also may mean the other person's acknowledgement of wrongdoing and commitment to change.

If we encounter *rejection*, we will not be able to move toward trust. Rejection moves us toward *injury* again. In some relationships, such rejection and repeated injury leads to the extreme form of *withdrawal*, that is, to *exit* from the relationship. Again we need to consider the injury in the relationship and its meaning for us.

At some point we experience *healing* and a stronger sense of self. We consider what *risk* we are able to take. Given our past experience with a particular person we experienced as abusive, we take risks in new relationships with different people. If we find acceptance there, we can regain *trust*.

As stated, there are conditions which may make forgiveness possible. The church community plays a valuable role in the provision of such conditions, which take time and effort.

The survivor needs to experience justice as a part of the healing process. This happens when the survivor's story of abuse is listened to and believed, when opportunity is provided to heal, and when the offender is called to accountability.

Restitution is one extremely valuable step in justice-making. Restitution generally involves a financial payment by the offender to the victim. It is a concrete symbol of the offender's willingness to acknowledge responsibility for the harm done.

While this occurs infrequently in domestic abuse, it is one step churches can promote as they attempt to make justice.

One unusual example of reconciliation and restitution, involving abuse in a large institution was reported in the Canadian press in the summer of 1992.

Over 400 former students of two Ontario Catholic-run training schools reported sexual and physical abuse at those schools. Rather than pursue the traditional legal avenues for redress, these former students formed an association called Helpline to deal with the aftermath of the abuse.

Helpline approached the various parties involved and, over a period of twenty months, they conducted negotiations with the responsible parties (The Brothers of the Christian Schools of Ottawa, the Government of Ontario, and the Catholic Archdioceses of Ottawa and Toronto). Mediators assisted the process.

Through the negotiations, the parties were able to arrive at a Reconciliation Model Agreement designed to help heal the impact of abuse and to encourage restoration of the victims' lost trust in the spiritual and secular institutions of society.

The agreement provided for a flexible program to address the specific needs of each individual. Key features included—

- counseling;
- apologies;
- financial compensation to validated claimants;
- additional compensation for pain and suffering;
- funding for medical/dental needs, vocational rehabilitation, education upgrading, and literacy training needs.
- contributions toward wage loss.
- the appointment of a recorder to publish the experiences of former students wishing to be heard and to make recommendations designed to prevent abuse in institutional settings;
- a commitment by both government and church to eradicate child abuse from society through a series of preventive measures, including research and public education.

This agreement is a powerful vision of how responsible parties can offer concrete aids to heal survivors.

5. *We acknowledge the distinction between forgiveness and reconciliation.*

Forgiveness precedes reconciliation. Reconciliation may or may not follow forgiveness. Reconciliation—the restoration to just and caring family relationships—may not be possible or healthy.

Our acts of forgiveness occur in the context of time and

space. We cannot turn back the clock and give the child an abuse-free childhood; the chance for that parent to tenderly care for that child is gone. The battered wife may have endured too many years of abuse to permit her to move back into a marital relationship with her spouse, even if he has changed his ways. Either the offender or the survivor may have died or be unavailable for the relationship.

God Heals in Different Ways

Many survivors choose a time of separation from their offenders (as noted earlier in this chapter and chapter 5) and discover that this separation is an essential condition for their healing. We need to walk alongside survivors as they determine the appropriate level of relationship with their offender.

A survivor may forgive his offender but the offender's refusal to acknowledge wrongdoing prohibits harmony from developing. The survivor may then experience internal reconciliation without experiencing relationship reconciliation.

An offender may experience God's forgiveness and may be able to forgive herself. But her victim may still be working through the hurt and the hate and not be able to open himself to a relationship. The offender may then find internal reconciliation, hoping for the day when her victim can consider relating to her. Offenders who acknowledge their wrongdoing and demonstrate their willingness to turn from their sin pave the way for reconciliation.

At all times it is important to remember that it is the violence that has destroyed the covenant. The victim should not be blamed.

On some occasions, both survivors and offenders may be ready to be reconciled. When this occurs we thank God for the demonstration of healing grace. We do not assume that this is what must happen in all situations and push ourselves and others toward it. Rather, by submitting to a process of healing, we accept God's gracious touch wherever we receive it.

* * * * * * * * * *

Victoria worked at her healing by speaking to church groups, pastors, women's sewing circles, and youth meetings. She shared her experience with abuse and how it affected her faith.

She often said, "I will never forgive my father. How do you forgive a man like that?" He never admitted his guilt and went on to abuse many other girls and women.

Still, in Victoria's speaking engagements, she met offenders. Although she initially feared them, she told her story to them and listened to them tell their stories. Once she participated in a pastors' workshop, sharing the platform with an offender. Afterward she remarked, "In the future, I want to tell my story at the same time as an offender. I think it's important that people hear the story from both sides."

While unable to forgive her father, Victoria continued to open herself to forgiveness, healing, and reconciliation by her attitudes toward other offenders.

Prayer
Dear God,

You offer the gift of forgiveness to free us from past hurts. Open our hearts to your healing. Nudge us toward gracious compassion for those who have wounded us. Grant us patience to listen to our sisters and brothers who are survivors of family violence. May they find a way to move past the anger and bitterness, into healing and wholeness. Amen.

Discussion Questions
1. What have been your experiences with forgiveness? (They may or may not relate to examples of family violence.) Relate your response to Figure 1 (below) if possible. Note any differences between times when you are the offender and when you are the victim.

2. Where have you experienced others pushing you into forgiveness prior to your being ready?

3. Consider whether your own uneasiness with the pain and anger (the hurt and hate) of family violence causes you to push forgiveness prematurely. How can you be more patient with your own discomfort so others do not feel pushed by you?

4. Victoria's father has just asked to become a member of your church, which is also Victoria's church. You are a pastor or a member of the pastoral team that processes membership requests. You know from Victoria that he has never acknowledged his sin, and that their relationship is severed because of his abuse and refusal to take responsibility for it. What is your response to him?

Resources

Fortune, Marie M., "Forgiveness: The Last Step," *Violence in the Family*.

Heggen, Carolyn Holderread, "Repentance, Restitution, Forgiveness, and Reconciliation," *Sexual Abuse in Christian Families and Churches*.

Smedes, Lewis B., *Forgive and Forget: Healing the Hurts You Don't Deserve*.

Cycle of Relationship

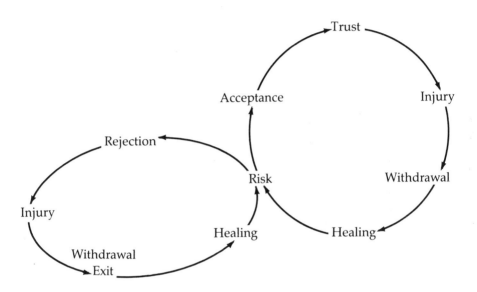

(adapted from a model by Ron Kraybill and used by permission)

13

Full Circle: Benefits of Facing Family Power Issues

"WHAT'S THE DIFFERENCE between physical abuse and correction?" my father inquired as I was working on this manuscript.

"That's a good question," I replied, as I considered many possible answers. "It seems the more we know about how physical punishment affects children, the more it is considered an unhealthy and wrong way to discipline."

Dad moved to personal reflection, as he readily does. "I know my anger got in the way when I was smacking my children. So I made myself a rule—three hits, then stop. That was my way of keeping the correction from becoming abusive."

There were too many emotions spinning inside me to continue carefully measured dialogue. I countered, "I didn't experience the spankings as helpful; I experienced them as damaging."

Our eyes made contact as we struggled to understand each other's words. Could we speak honestly? Could we trust our vulnerable places to each other? Could our anger and hurt guide us to better ways of relating? Could we be gracious and tender with each other? Would our openness to God's guiding hand lead us to new ways of being family?

* * * * * * * * * *

This book ends as it began, by flipping the coin of abusive family relationships to consider its opposite side—healthy family relationships. At this point, we do so with the knowledge of the abuse of power within families.

All of us can learn valuable lessons by educating ourselves about abuse in individual families. As we listen to the stories of people and families, we consider our own hurts and the experiences that are currently painful or are unresolved hurts from our childhoods. We also benefit from making connections between our own families, our hurting churches, and damaging societies.

Over and over again during the months that I worked on this manuscript, I heard comments that reflect this growing awareness of the connections between individuals, family violence, and larger systems.

"Each of us has a hurting child within. The survivor of family violence reminds us of our hurt child. We can respond to that inner hurt either by working toward its healing or by denying its existence."

"God is calling the church to renewal. Healing comes before renewal. We have to heal from the sin of oppressing women and children before God will bring about renewal."

"The layers of family violence are coming off like the layers of an onion. At the core is a betrayal of trust and an abuse of power. Only when men acknowledge the power they have just by virtue of their gender can they consciously change the way they relate to women."

These comments, all made by men, point us to the value of the current discussions on family violence for the potential healing each of us may find. In this chapter we consider how our families can be strengthened and made healthier and holier by the lessons we learn from power abuses within the family.

Lesson 1—Listen to each other.

The intensity and anguish that drives many survivors makes it nearly impossible for witnesses to ignore them. At the same time, survivors note that their healing begins and is encouraged by people who believe them. The best gift is one's whole and complete attention.

This same gift is meant to be shared in our intimate relationships. When we truly listen to each other, we demonstrate that we value the other person. When people feel valued, there is better communication. The bonds of love are more secure and conflicts are handled more readily. Energy can be directed outward as members use their gifts to share the love of God with others.

For too long, the voices of women and children have not been listened to or respected:

"Children should be seen and not heard."

"Women should obey their husbands without questioning their authority."

"A child who challenges his parents should be spanked until he learns respect."

Each of these statements attempts to control women and children, producing the opposite of healthy, nurtured family members. Sensitive listening allows all family member to grow to their fullest God-given potential.

Doris reflected on the language ability of her fourteen-month-old grandson, Miles. At a family dinner, she asked him, "Would you like more potatoes?"

He shook his head no.

"You don't like potatoes?" she queried.

Miles again tossed his blond head.

Doris concluded Miles' ability to communicate was related to the seriousness with which his parents listened to him. Because they did listen to him, he could clearly identify his "yea" and his "nay" at a very young age.

We all benefit from practicing the art of listening in our most intimate human connections. Remember: each person—from youngest to eldest, males and females, with whatever range of abilities—is created in the image of God. Each person bears witness to the presence of God in our midst.

Lesson 2—Share our stories.

By entering into the stories of family abuse, we learn about the value of sharing our stories with each other. When I hear another person's story, I compare it with mine. I seek both to make connections between the other's story and mine, and to learn more about how to live my life. The same possibility exists in family relationships.

David tells stories with the lively embellishments and voice changes typical of U.S. southerners. He credits this ability to his mother, Coffee, another great storyteller. David's father, George, is now suffering from the effects of a stroke, and David regrets that he never heard his dad tell personal stories. He missed the opportunity to truly know his father.

In response, David tries to share his stories with his family members. By doing so he hopes they will all benefit from the human bond that occurs when we share our stories.

A part of sharing our stories is telling our secrets. The untold secrets burden our hearts and build barriers between us, preventing us from truly knowing and loving each other. (There are, of course, some secrets meant to be kept between intimates or information that needs to be treated with the utmost care and dignity.)

Too often we hoard a secret out of fear or shame. As we are sharing our stories, we have the potential to loosen ourselves from fear and shame into the freedom of truth and intimate communication.

The following questions are examples of attempts to unearth family secrets:

"How were you affected by Grandpa's alcoholism?"

"What did those miscarriages mean for your mother?"

"How did people respond to his suicide?"

"What were you taught about sexuality? How did your understanding of sexuality relate to your development?"

Yes, these examples are intense (maybe even too hot to handle). But the more intensity around the secret, the more impact it already has had on the family and the greater potential for healing and intimacy if the secret can be told.

Lesson 3—Model the love of God.

The beauty of the Christian family is that it can offer a visible symbol of God's love. God's gracious, constant love surrounds us, protects us, accepts us, and guides us. In our intimate relationships, we have the opportunity to practice giving and receiving such love.

Our understanding of God's love is richly developed by considering Jesus. How did he understand power, love, and relationships? While we have discussed this in a number of chapters, it is worth repeating. Let us consider two additional passages that reflect on Jesus' demonstration of God's love.

In the first passage, we hear Mary, the mother of Jesus, respond with praise to the news of her pregnancy.

> My soul magnifies the Lord,
> And my spirit rejoices in God my Savior,
>   for he has looked with favor on the
> lowliness of his servant.
>   Surely, from now on all generations
> will call me blessed;
>   for the Mighty One has done great
> things for me, and holy is his name.
>   His mercy is for those who fear
> him from generation to generation.
>   He has shown strength with his arm;
> he has scattered the proud in
> the thoughts of their hearts.
>   He has brought down the powerful
> from their thrones,
>   and lifted up the lowly;
>   he has filled the hungry with good things,
>   and sent the rich away empty.
>   He has helped his servant Israel,
>   in remembrance of his mercy,
>   according to the promise he made
> to our ancestors,
>   to Abraham and to his descendants forever.
>   (Luke 1:46-55)

In the second passage the writer reflects on Jesus' use of power.

"Let the same mind be in you
that was in Christ Jesus,
   who, though he was the form
of God, did not regard equality with
God as something to be exploited,
   but emptied himself, taking
the form of a slave,
   being born in human likeness.
   And being found in human form,
he humbled himself
   and became obedient to the point
of death—
   even death on a cross."
      (Philippians 2:5-8)

These two passages bear witness to Jesus' use of power. In the first example, there is a great reversal—the proud, the powerful, and the rich are all overturned; the lowly and the hungry are satisfied. Jesus is a great leveler. His message points us to a world where there is justice, equality, and shared power for all. In the second passage, we learn how Jesus responded to his divine power—not by exploiting it, but by humbly identifying with those he came to serve. Turning these concepts back onto our family relationships, we can claim the Jesus way.

Power is to be shared. Power is not to be exploited or wielded in harsh, controlling ways. Those accorded the greater power (parents, men) must guard against exploiting their power. We need to recognize that God desires fair relationships. This means we reject systems which set one group *over* another. We seek systems where each person's contribution is valued and each person's voice is welcome.

Lesson 4—Love each other deeply.

One biblical writer invites us to "maintain constant love for one another, for love covers a multitude of sins" (1 Pet. 4:8).

Love—this wonderful, nourishing, restoring emotion, given by God. God *is* love.

We experience love in our family relationships, and we also open our hearts to God's love to guide and strengthen our relationships.

Henri was treated horribly by his father. For years he knew only abuse—physical, sexual, and emotional—from his father. Henri found meaning in his Christian walk and struggled to heal from his damaged childhood.

He sought to close off the abusive part of his past by naming to his father what he appreciated from him. As he searched he realized there was only one thing. His dad, incapacitated by Alzheimer's, could not enter into a conversation. But Henri told him anyhow. "Dad, thank you for giving me the gift of life. Thank you for being the vehicle by which I entered the world." That was it. Everything else he received from his dad had been destructive.

Still this step enabled Henri to move on in his relationship with his father. Henri and his wife decided to renovate their home to provide a safe place for the ailing father to live out his final days.

Henri's story is not everyone's story. All survivors will not be led to precisely the same responses. But our openness to God's love will heal us. Love covers a multitude of sins.

Summary

Our children and intimate loved ones force us to confront our own evil. They crack open our hearts, and we see the good and the bad. We choose. Will we harden our hearts and continue the abuse, setting in motion suffering which ripples out over the generations? Or will we repent of our sins and ask God for new hearts?

I am still learning to follow Jesus in my family relationships. I learn much from the survivors and offenders who share their stories of brokenness and restoration with me. I learn much from the Spirit's gentle, persistent nudging in my heart.

My father and I work away at it. He offered helpful words when he said, "I would like you to experience resolution of your past hurts." When I said I would like him to listen, he agreed that he would listen.

I asked him about his experiences with his parents. He readily shared his story in ways that helped me understand him better.

His actions as a responsive, sensitive parent demonstrated his desire not to exploit his power but to use it carefully, in ways that empower me and others. He and I both seek to remain open to the love of God which covers a multitude of sins.

In my roles of spouse and parent, I too am challenged. My son tells me, "I don't like it when you yell at me. It hurts my ears." I allow harsh words to tumble from my mouth in an argument with my husband. I use my power in cruel ways.

I repent. I return to the lessons. Listen. Share stories. Model the love of God. Love deeply.

There is hope.

Prayer
Dear God,
Open our hearts. Fill us with courage and strength and compassion. Guide our family relationships so that we may model your love in our actions. Amen.

Discussion Questions
1. What have you learned about the abuse of power in the family during your study of this book?
2. What stories would you like to hear from your family members? What stories would you like to share with family members?
3. How has your understanding of your own power in family relationships been affected during this study? What changes do you want to make in how you use your power?
4. How do you give and receive the love of God in your family relationships, and in your relationships with your church community?

How to Use This Book

CONGRATULATIONS! Take a moment to affirm the individual or group who has decided it is important for your congregation to educate themselves about family violence. It is not easy to look squarely at this difficult and widespread tragedy, so you are to be commended for taking the first step.

This book was conceived for use in small group settings in churches. Adult Sunday school classes, elders and deacons groups, small fellowship groups, and ministerial fellowships are possible settings. The book is written with the average church person in mind, meaning that attempts were made to keep the material as clear and readable as possible.

Even so, given the intense feelings associated with both the abuse of power within the family and this author's approach to the subject, the group leader may find the task challenging. The following is written to make the challenge more manageable.

1. If possible, find a coleader for support and strengthening. You and the group will benefit if two individuals are working together to lead the discussion and debrief and plan sessions. If you do not have a coleader, try to arrange for someone to be a consultant you can turn to for post-session reflection and pre-session planning.

2. Read each chapter well in advance of the discussion. Prepare for careful presentation of material you imagine might be sensitive for your group.

3. Set a tone in the group that frees people to share comfortably or be silent. Avoid blaming and criticizing, and expect others to do so, even when they disagree. Expect people to practice good listening skills.

4. Be aware that the topics addressed in this book can evoke powerful emotions. Plan in advance how you will address such responses by offering a calm, accepting presence.

5. Know that there are people in your group who have direct experience with family violence. Address this at the beginning of the group and possibly at the beginning of each session. Make comments such as "I know from my reading material that there are individuals here who have either been survivors or offenders of family violence. Please know that as a church community we wish to help you. We will try in our discussion to address your issues in ways you will experience as healing rather than offensive."

If survivors or perpetrators of abuse have identified themselves, arrange for someone to check in with them regularly to see how they are managing in the group. Do they need additional support? Would it be helpful for them to tell the group their story? Do they need permission to withdraw from the group if it is too difficult to participate?

6. The discussion questions are intended to help the group debrief the chapter and consider how the book relates to your church setting. You may also want to allow for some other kinds of questions at the beginning or end of each session: like, "What struck you about this chapter?" or "What feelings do you have after reading this chapter?" or "How are you feeling as we end the group today?"

7. Be prepared for defensive or even hostile reactions; such individuals are likely having tender wounds activated. Reflective responses, like "It sounds like you're very upset by that," or "You seem to feel quite angry" may be useful. Acknowledge the individual's perspective.

Do not allow one person to dominate the discussion. If you

are unsuccessful in limiting the person by simple acknowledgment of his or her perspective, then firmly say, "I don't want to take any more of the group time on this topic. Perhaps you and I can discuss it after the session."

8. Consider having an outside resource person address the group. Possibly a survivor or offender would be willing to tell his or her story. Or a professional could bring additional insight and information to the group.

Bibliography

Alsdurf, James and Phyllis Alsdurf, *Battered into Submission: The Tragedy of Wife Abuse in the Christian Home*, Downers Grove, Ill.: InterVarsity, 1989.
A brief, informative book that challenges the church to examine its role in addressing wife battering.

Bass, Ellen and Laura Davis, *The Courage to Heal*, New York: Harper & Row, 1988.
The authors gently guide female survivors of childhood sexual abuse toward healing. Also helpful for male survivors. (It should be noted that the book's guidelines for identifying abuse have been criticized for being too simplistic and potentially leading to false memory syndrome.)

Block, Isaac, *Assault on God's Image: Domestic Abuse*, Winnipeg, Man.: Windflower Communications, 1992.
Block's research on domestic abuse among Mennonites signals how widespread and serious the issues are.

Blume, E. Sue, *Secret Survivors: Uncovering Incest and Its Aftereffects in Women*, New York: John Wiley and Sons, 1990.
Clearly describes the long-term effects of incest, explaining the

coping responses of survivors as necessary, logical, and protective.

Brewer, Connie, *Escaping the Shadows, Seeking the Light,* New York: HarperCollins, 1991.
A dozen individuals share their stories as Christians recovering from childhood sexual abuse.

Brueggeman, Walter, *Praying the Psalms,* Winona, Minn.: St. Mary's Press, 1986.
This eloquent theologian writes of the power of the Psalms and the need to lament.

Carnes, Patrick, *Out of the Shadows,* Minneapolis: CompCare Publishers, 1989.
Carnes gives insights into the individual whose sexual abuse has an addictive component. Also helpful for survivors who experience sexual addiction.

Colorosa, Barbara, *Video—Winning at Parenting . . . Without Beating Your Kids,* Kids Are Worth It!, P O Box 621108, Littleton, CO 80162.
An excellent resource to teach the appropriate use of natural consequences.

Crary, Elizabeth, *Without Spanking or Spoiling: A Practical Approach to Toddler and Preschool Guidance,* Seattle: Parenting Press, 1979.
An excellent, practical resource on parenting without the use of physical punishment.

Davis, Laura, *Allies in Healing,* New York: Harper & Row, 1991.
Using a question-and-answer format, Davis offers information and counsel to the friends and family of incest survivors.

Evert, Kathy and Inie Bijkerk, *When You're Ready: A Woman's Healing from Childhood Physical and Sexual Abuse by Her Mother,* Walnut Creek, Calif.: Launch Press, 1988.
A powerful and revealing story.

Faber, Adele and Elaine Mazlish, *How to Talk So Kids Will Listen and Listen So Kids Will Talk*, New York: Avon, 1980.
An invaluable guide to develop nurturing, empowering communication skills. Very easy to read with cartoon illustrations.

Fortune, Marie Marshall, *Clergy Misconduct: Sexual Abuse in the Ministerial Relationship*, The Center for the Prevention of Sexual and Domestic Violence, 1992.
This excellent material addresses clergy sexual misconduct. It assists us in identifying and understanding power in our relationships, which enables us to use our power more justly and carefully.

_____, *Keeping the Faith: Questions and Answers for the Abused Woman*, New York: Harper & Row, 1987.
Extremely encouraging resource for the battered Christian woman.

_____, *Sexual Abuse Prevention: A Study for Teenagers*, New York: United Church Press.
A curriculum intended for use with religious youth groups. A leader's guide.

_____, *Sexual Violence: The Unmentionable Sin*, New York, Pilgrim Press, 1983.
This initial work by Fortune continues to inform the church's response to sexual violence.

_____, *Violence in the Family*, Cleveland, Ohio: Pilgrim Press, 1991.
Packed with lots of useful information including material on battering, and the pastoral response to family violence. Geared to clergy.

Frank, Jan, *A Door of Hope*, San Bernadino, Calif.: Here's Life Publishers, 1987.
Frank writes from her experience as an incest victim, and offers steps of healing for Christians.

Greven, Philip, *Spare the Child: The Religious Roots of Punishment and the Psychological Impact of Physical Abuse*, New York: Knopf, 1991.
A thorough and disturbing analysis of the physical punishment of children.

Heggen, Carolyn Holderread, *Sexual Abuse in Christian Homes and Churches*, Scottdale, Pa.: Herald Press, 1993.
Excellent psychological, spiritual, and societal analysis.

Keene, Jane A., *A Winter's Song: A Liturgy for Women Seeking Healing from Childhood Sexual Abuse*, New York: Pilgrim Press, 1991.
A powerful resource to aid a survivor's spiritual healing.

Kraybill, Donald, *The Upside-Down Kingdom*, rev. ed., Scottdale, Pa.: Herald Press, 1990.
The revolutionary call of Jesus in the synoptic Gospels.

Lew, Michael, *Victims No Longer*, New York: Harper & Row, 1988.
A compassionate guide for men recovering from childhood sexual abuse.

Poling, James Newton, *The Abuse of Power: A Theological Problem*, Nashville: Abingdon, 1991.
Using sexual abuse as the context, Poling offers theological insights into the abuse of power. He tackles tough questions and offers hopeful directions.

Reid, Kathryn Goering with Marie M. Fortune, *Preventing Child Sexual Abuse: A Curriculum for Children Ages 9-12*, New York: United Church Press, 1989.
A curriculum for use in Christian education.

Rutter, Peter, *Sex in the Forbidden Zone*, New York: Ballantine, 1989.
Deals with sexual abuse of women by male professionals. Offers helpful information about males who cross sexual boundaries.

Sanford, Linda Tschirhart and Mary Ellen Donovan, *Women and Self-Esteem*, New York: Penguin, 1984.
Written for women, useful for men as well, particularly as we consider how we can nurture the self-esteem of others.

Smedes, Lewis B., *Forgive and Forget: Healing the Hurts We Don't Deserve*, New York: Simon and Schuster, Inc., 1984.
Despite the title, this is a helpful exploration of forgiveness, which Smedes describes as an "art" and a "gift from God."

Sonkin, Daniel J. and Michael Durphy, *Learning to Live Without Violence*, San Francisco: Volcano Press, 1989.
A manual for men who are working to control their violent behavior. Useful exercises for anyone who wants to deal with anger more effectively.

Trible, Phyllis, *Texts of Terror*, Philadelphia: Fortress, 1984.
Trible's meticulous critique is thorough, challenging, and well worth the effort for those who want to understand these difficult texts from the Hebrew Scripture.

Weems, Renita J., *Just a Sister Away*, San Diego: LuraMedia, 1988.
Offers a womanist vision of women's relationships in the Bible.

Wisechild, Louise M., *She Who Was Lost Is Remembered: Healing from Incest Through Creativity*, Seattle, Wash.: Seal Press, 1991.
The title accurately conveys the power of this book. Awakens the creativity of wounded persons.

Yantzi, Mark, *Sexual Offending and Restoration,* Scottdale, Pa.: Herald Press, 1998.
Provides perspectives and interaction of victims and offenders, and new hope for those affected.

The Author

MELISSA A. MILLER has been a counselor at Shalom Counselling Services (Kitchener, Ont.) since 1985. She has extensive experience working with issues of family violence. An author and public speaker, Miller is a popular leader of workshops on such themes as family life, sexuality, family violence, and self-esteem.

In 1981 Miller received an MASC in applied psychology from the University of Waterloo. She received her B.A. in psychology from Eastern Mennonite College (Harrisonburg, Va.) in 1976. She is a clinical member of the American Association of Marriage and Family Therapy.

Born in Pennsylvania, Miller has lived in Ontario with her husband, Dean Peachey, since 1978. They are parents of Daniel (1986). Their church home is Mannheim Mennonite, where Miller has served through preaching and worship leading and also as an elder and youth Sunday school teacher.